Dr. Franklin Bray has found effective ways to overcome fear—be it the fear of God, of failure, of sin, of temptation, or other. In this scholarly and pastoral presentation, he reveals principles that, if applied, will deliver the fearful. In this spiritual exploration, Dr. Bray draws from his experience as a pastor and a clinical psychotherapist to expose fear and how to conquer it, opening the door to liberation in these times of great uncertainty.

—Dr. Clarence Pamphile, ordained minister of religion, author, college lecturer

Dr. Bray's book is an excellent guide to help anyone who wants to build a practical relationship with God. He seems to unhinge the many questions that you may be asking about the practicality of establishing that workable relationship by "re-presenting" God to his readers, possibly in a way that Christianity in general has not.

Bray seeks to make a case to vindicate the character of God and presents Him as a loving God and not the God who may have been portrayed by Christianity throughout the years. As such, he provides a tangible and practical guide to seeing and experiencing God.

Get ready to be taken on a journey that will provide you with step-by-step guidelines, almost like a GPS, safely routing you to your destination: heaven!

—Dr. Nadine Collins, author and spiritual wellness coach

In this text, Dr. Bray has invited us to consider how this deeply human emotional experience—fear—affects every area of our lives. He is an able guide for his readers and can assist them on their journeys toward spiritual wholeness.

—Bishop James H. Evans Jr., PhD, LittD, president and professor of systematic theology, emeritus, Colgate Rochester Crozer Divinity School

Fearless!
Breaking Through
Barriers
in Your Walk with
GOD

Dr. Franklin A. Bray Sr, DMin

WESTBOW
PRESS®
A DIVISION OF THOMAS NELSON
& ZONDERVAN

WestBow Press books may be ordered through booksellers or by contacting:

WestBow Press
A Division of Thomas Nelson & Zondervan
1663 Liberty Drive
Bloomington, IN 47403
www.westbowpress.com
844-714-3454

ISBN: 978-1-6642-5876-1 (sc)
ISBN: 978-1-6642-5878-5 (hc)
ISBN: 978-1-6642-5877-8 (e)

Library of Congress Control Number: 2022903395

Print information available on the last page.

WestBow Press rev. date: 05/19/2023

To my sons, Franklin A. and Fareed A. Bray. This work will serve to enhance your journey with God. I committed myself to the will of God and desire that you'd do the same. Secondly, to every committed or struggling spiritual sojourner, known or unknown, note that you're not alone on your journey or in your struggle. Your triumph awaits your conquests. To every victor, keep excelling. To every spectator, your journey awaits your consent. To every survivor of human indignities, systemic or nonsystemic, I urge you to live with the sincere consciousness of God in your heart. You will triumph. For all I pray that the Creator of this and other worlds will acknowledge your sincerity and provide you with much-needed guidance and support every step of your spiritual journey.

CONTENTS

ACKNOWLEDGMENTS

I am eternally grateful for the contribution of countless individuals for supporting my way through the journey of this text. The editorial assistance of West Bow Press and Vera and Matthew Hunte must be cited. It was critical to have them help me say "it" well. My family for their unwavering support and "keeping it real" feedback on the presentation of the idea to publish. I pay special gratitude to friends and colleagues such as Dr. Kern Tobias of Caribbean Union Conference of SDA, Dr. Jeffrey Brown, editor of *Ministry Magazine*, Dr. Clarence Pamphile, Dr. Nadine Collins, and Dr. James Evans for their critiques, reviews, and gratuitous words. You added inspiration to the journey. Thank you.

Those who wait for perfect weather will never plant seeds; those who look at every cloud will never harvest crops.

Ecclesiastes 11:4 (NCV)

FOREWORD

Dr. Franklin Bray's *Fearless* shares the compelling journey of the author as he deals with the difference between the fear of God and the fear for God. As a theologian, Bray is eminently qualified to treat with this perplexing issue, and he has justified the effort.

This important work is a mixture of scholarship and deep spiritual thought. Readers will enjoy the simplification of the Hebrew word study and the way the discoveries are applied to real-life situations. The references to his own experiences allow readers to understand the author much better and realize why this topic is so relevant and important.

Fear of God is to be afraid of Him, and fear for God is to have respect for Him. The author explains this difference as cowardice versus reverence, and he strikes a beautiful balance in the way one should relate to God. It is important to note that "a truly successful life is founded on fear of God. biblical wisdom literature clearly emphasizes that the fear of the Lord is the beginning of wisdom. Because to fear God is to know Him, and to know Him is to fear Him. It is that medium that motivates a relationship of praise and adoration to God."

It is exciting to observe the contribution that Dr. Bray is making in the lives of the readers, especially in the climate of fear during the COVID-19 pandemic. There is a general feeling of anxiety and stress among many people, and to have a correct understanding of the character of God is essential.

Respect for God requires sincerity, transparency, contrition, and humility. These dispositions reflect one's understanding of God's majesty and the limitation of humankind. The reader will experience these dispositions and will be moved to respect and revere God while not being afraid of Him or taking Him as a casual friend.

Aristotle said, "Men are swayed more of fear than by reverence." However, it is reassuring to note the following scripture:

There is no fear in love; but perfect love casts out fear, because fear involves torment. But he who fears has not be made perfect in love. (1 John 4:18 NKJV)

Enjoy this gift from Dr. Franklin Bray and God.

—Dr. Kern Tobias
President, Caribbean Union Conference of Seventh-day Adventist

PROLOGUE

She sat quietly, quite alert, in the lobby, close to the coffee table. He was happy to see her, and they embraced, providing each other much-anticipated comfort.

"I'm glad to see you again," she whispered with the looks of a charmer.

"I am delighted as well," he exclaimed, quickly casting his eyes to the leather couch nestled in the crowd.

"So, how long have you been here?" she asked.

"I've been waiting to distract you from your motivational self," he muttered, ensuring that he was gazing straight into her eyes.

"Well, I'm here now," she stated as she took a step toward him.

"Won't you even ask me my name?" he asked.

"Oh! Aren't you my friend, Fear?" She smiled.

"Of course I am. Haven't changed my name since we last met." He chuckled.

"Then I'm not afraid. I know deception when I see it. Its expression is so predictable. I know you, and I know what you can do." She smiled broadly and placed her left hand across his right shoulder. "Come on. Let me walk you to your car."

Where there is reverence, there is fear, but there is not reverence everywhere that there is fear because fear presumably has a wider extension than reverence.

—Socrates

INTRODUCTION

Life is a spiritual journey. It is the quest to satisfy the curious space naturally made available at birth. Life is an encounter with forces that are either captivating to our unique preferences or our desire to choose our preferences. Everything we do or say, everywhere we go, whatever we eat or drink, what friendships we develop, what thoughts we conjure about the things we see, taste, feel, hear, or smell are all influenced by universal elements that are beyond our finiteness. Within all of our thoughts and feelings are the elements of imperfection that will influence the trajectory of our lives. We are caught, therefore, in an existential passage from birth to the grave that will provide varying experiences with pleasant and not so pleasant features. Our expectations of what should be and what we want will bend to the powers of universal laws and structures, all within the hands of God.

Humankind, therefore, is linked to God without their participation in the creation process. Without consultation or confirmation of humankind's desire to be part of the universal composition of all things, seen or unseen, God, the Great Mover, God the Creator of all things, tangible and intangible, God the Establisher of all things perfect for the survival of all creation, sets all things in motion for His creation. Consequently, it is imperative that humankind recognizes how the universality of our humanity, its link to the eternality of God, the existence of the universe—and hence who we are—are all impacted by universal laws.

For the purposes of this text, I will introduce two of the many universal laws that I have discovered to be evident in the operations of this world. They are the *law of curiosity* and the *law of worship*. Both of these laws are supportive of who God is, His infinite authority, His unlimited power, and His eternal presence.

The thought of God might be foreign to anyone who does not believe that God exists or painfully disturbing to another who used to believe in the possibility of God only later to disappointedly conclude "there is no

God" or "God is dead." Strangely, many people struggle with such religious realities.

Here is a classic example. Friedrich Nietzsche, born in 1844, in the rural southwest of Leipzig, Germany, with both father and grandfathers as Lutheran ministers, had a strongly religious childhood. After Nietzsche lost his father at the early age of four years to a brain ailment, the family moved to nearby Naumburg an der Saale. At twenty years old, he studied theology and philology—the interpretation of classical and biblical texts—at the University of Bonn. At twenty-one, he enrolled at the University of Leipzig, familiarizing himself with the work of Arthur Schopenhauer, whose atheistic viewpoints seem to have inspired Nietzsche's departure from his conservative religious upbringing.

He struggled with the disparity between the denunciation of Christianity and atheism (his understanding that God is not). In writing his first real criticisms of Christianity, he posited that Christian values constituted a mechanism to compel individual conformity to something that was disadvantageous and corrupting of good character. Nietzsche called for humanity to crucify orthodox morality, which he deemed superstitious:

> Do we not hear the noise of the grave-diggers who are burying God? Do we not smell the divine putrefaction?—for even Gods putrefy! God is dead. God remains dead. And we have killed him. How shall we comfort ourselves, the murderers of all murderers? What was holiest and mightiest of all that the world has yet owned has bled to death under our knives: who will wipe this blood off us? What water is there for us to clean ourselves? What festivals of atonement, what sacred games shall we have to invent? Is not the greatness of this deed too great for us? Must we ourselves not become gods simply to appear worthy of it?

Perhaps the ultimate irony for Frederic Nietzsche, a man who had devoted much of his adult life to attacking Christianity, was that his sister arranged a Christian funeral for him—followed by burial in the family gravesite beside his hometown church.

Like Nietzsche, with a denunciation of God, many have impressions of a universal power that influences their life's advancement or the exactness of their mortality. Others would prefer to say, "I don't know if there is a God. What I do know is that there is something or someone out there that seems to be keeping things in order or else unfathomable chaos would have already broken loose down here." Yet many more would acknowledge that somewhere within the consciousness of humanity is the silent desire to worship. The law of worship spans the universe and is linked to the law of curiosity. Who or what should I worship? What benefit is to be derived from the worshipping of such power or person? How do I know when my worship is appreciated or is in congruence with the expectations of such power or person?

God as a dominant authority is unsettling to humankind. Fear of a satisfactory relationship and balance of power disturbs many. Fear drives the desired relationship with God or the struggle to acknowledge the need or the desire for spiritual growth. This too spans the globe. It is the bombardment of such thought that further fuels fear, which provides no spiritual reprieve until the soul is satisfied that it has appeased a supernatural power. That desire motivates humankind's search for actualization, piety, and a spiritual consciousness that can fill the vacuum created at birth.

I will not seek to provide a theological dissertation here on proof that God is or seek to dissuade you from searching for Him. The law of curiosity is motivated by major principles, including honesty, objectivity, teachability, humility, and tenacity. In my search for life's meaning, I discovered no one can satisfy your vacuum for worship but you and that you can only do it when you aptly apply the principles of the law of curiosity.

On a very personal level, I have discovered that there have been and will always be times that will test the soul. Many are ill prepared for the challenges that conflict with our agendas and are therefore being forced to recalibrate our future plans and find the necessary courage and flexibility to improvise our days. At such times, we seek a spiritual fortress where nothing but certainty and tranquility are in abundance. In a very personal way, those times have led me to discover God in a very reassuring way.

I have had to debunk many of the idiosyncrasies of God fed to me by significant others in my childhood. I have come to understand that I need to complete my spiritual journey with greater awareness than when I started and with greater depth than I felt necessary earlier on the journey. God, for me, is more than a universal phantom, a cosmic power, or a mysterious being. I believe God is personal in relationships, inclusive, and committed to the expansion and elevation of all humanity. This happens through the open door of worship. God is not dead, and He deserves to be worshipped.

So, you want to walk with God but you're afraid? Scared? Petrified? Teetering? So fearful that you don't know how to best manage your desire to know Him?

News flash! Everyone who gets into a relationship with God will ask the questions that you are now asking. Quite honestly, the concerns that you are raising are part of a larger pool of questions that "wannabe" Christians have raised with "already-being" Christians and sometimes have left disappointed because some "already-being" Christians are serving God out of fear (being afraid) and not out of reverence (respect and adoration).

So, you're not alone. I have been at those different stops on my spiritual journey at various seasons in my conversion experience. To the chagrin of many, when reflected in my behavior were issues that, according to dissenting voices, "raised in the church" Christians should not be struggling with, the response is still today what it has been. "Father, forgive them for they know not what they say. Self, focus on growth and not distraction. Self, don't give in to your fears. Get up and keep going. Your destination awaits you."

Sojourner, you are not alone on this journey. Many struggle with spiritual fears and others live daily, hoping that at some time in the not-too-distant future, they will overcome their fears and embrace a fresh perspective of who God is. Unfortunately, they are being derailed with misinformation about God.

Untruths about the character of God contribute majorly to a terrifying view of who He is. God is understood by some to be adversarial to his own creation using the tactic of fear and the threat of ultimate annihilation to safeguard adoration of Him. All creation is controlled through that mechanism, hence the deranging and paralyzing grip of fear in the soul of humankind. Still others believe that fear is an emotion, used as an instrument to create equilibrium in creation, and can be managed by anyone who has developed sufficient bravery to recognize its vicious attack on our growth and stability.

The opinion that God is vindictive, unfair, and operating as a despot has troubling consequences for any relationship that is to be formed between humans and God. Humankind is limited and therefore must decide to trust God and believe in His omniscience, omnipotence, omnipresence, infallibility, and eternalness or live in disagreement or neutrality with God's authenticity. The struggle is real and is impacted by fear.

Battling fear is not novel to anyone who desires to walk with God. It was commonplace before you and will be after you have exited life's stage. Some of the most notable characters in biblical history wrestled with fear yet attained phenomenal success in their spiritual lives. Others succumbed to the onslaught of the adversary. The solution for fear in your walk with God is in an earnest examination of your beliefs of who He is, which is in turn shaped by your absorption and application of relevant scriptural positions of the manifestation of God's power in your life and the lives of others. Nothing else can suffice.

Still hesitant about getting started on your much-needed journey? Maybe you started the spiritual journey and for reasons unexplainable to both you and others, you have discontinued the walk. It may be because something about your decision or the journey seems surreal or impossible. It may be that you're not sure of what motivated you to get started in the first place but what you know is that you're not "feeling" it right now.

Please allow me to assist you in getting ready for this journey. This book is going to provide you with practical navigational points to facilitate a much-anticipated triumphant walk. No one begins a journey with complete knowledge of all possible difficulties. The wise sojourner possesses a realistic plan on how to navigate possible mishaps while still maintaining a focus on their ultimate destination.

Our journey with God begins with the same principle *except* we have been guaranteed the presence and support of God every step of the way. How do you walk that road, day after day, year after year, decade after decade, facing new challenges every waking moment? It is completely impossible to do so without an acknowledgment that you were birthed to make a universal statement uniquely carved by you and that your voice is the personal channel through which that message can flow, the only instrument that no one but you can uniquely sound.

Your uniqueness was ordained by God to complement your spiritual journey. You will benefit from appreciation of God and of others. So, pay less attention to your daily necessities on this journey. Self-focus is disadvantageous to this journey's experiences. Note that God is the constant companion for the entire journey:

> A man that hath friends must shew himself friendly: and there is a friend that sticketh closer than a brother. (Proverbs 18:24 AKJV)

> God is your Protector all along your journey; When you pass through the waters, I will be with you; and when you pass through the rivers, they will not sweep over you. When you walk through the fire, you will not be burned; the flames will not set you ablaze. (Jeremiah 43:2 NIV)

Therefore, the journey will only be successful when, along the way, an honest dialogue is kept with your companion. It is important because:

> Fear of God stops humankind from acknowledging Him for who He is.
> Fear of God creates for humankind a picture of who God is not.
> Fear of God promotes a surface relationship with no heartfelt devotion.
> Fear of God is no different to fear of a beast.
> Fear of God extracts from repentance the deep-needed sorrow for sin.
> Fear of God promotes behavior modification and not heart transformation.
> Fear of God authenticates form without substance

The perception of who God is and how He interacts with humankind matters significantly. This book highlights the need for a more appropriate lexicon that will embrace the original intent of the word *fear*, thereby conveying a full expression of an authentic relationship with God. To fear God should be "to know Him." To know God is to understand the limitations of our understanding of who He is. Fear, therefore, is an appropriate response where there is no relationship with what is or what is to come. Fear loses its authenticity when knowledge of now and the future is in a relationship that you and I possess. Walking with God, therefore, bears no fear. I, therefore, implore you to authenticate your walk with God by accepting your limitations, including any selfish motivation to serve Him. Let the soul of your humanity manifest its truest character instead of seeking to relive the recorded lives of ancient biblical characters. Come on, let's begin the journey!

Fearless! Breaking Through Barriers In Your Walk With God

CHAPTER 1

God and Fear

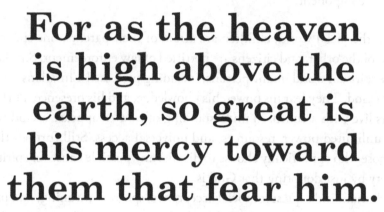

For as the heaven is high above the earth, so great is his mercy toward them that fear him.

—Psalm 103:11 (AKJV)

Many people live fearful lives. Humanity's fear is of something (unemployment, homelessness, loneliness, separation, divorce) or for something (family, marriage, friendship, or anything considered valuable for comfortable living).

For many, fear is engrained in the psyche from childhood. To the question of intergenerational adaptation of anxiety and fear, Dr. William R. Clark (March 6, 2000), professor emeritus in the Department of Molecular,

Cell, and Developmental Biology at the University of California, Los Angeles, and author of a number of popular books, offered the following response as reported in *Scientific American*:

> There is considerable evidence in humans, derived largely from studies of adopted children, and identical and fraternal twins reared together or apart, that a tendency toward anxiety and fear is a heritable trait. The specific form that fear takes phobias with specific associations, such as snakes, fear of pain, or of heights or closed spaces is almost entirely associated with individual environmental experiences. But the tendency to develop fearful or anxious responses to the environment in general has a clear genetic component.

In the social world, children are afraid of their parents, one spouse is afraid of the other, and citizens are petrified of law enforcement. Similarly, in the spiritual world, many persons, including professed Christians, live in fear of God. They fear his power, his knowledge, and his presence. Further, others live with a confused understanding of how to appease a God with such unlimited power, resources, and universal access. Still further, there are those who agnostically choose to dismiss any possible cause for spiritual anxiety by just doubting that God is.

Humankind's quest for social acceptance, spiritual meaning, and piety is deeply hampered by a fear of God, the misnomer of an unmatched, unfair power. A misconception of who God is, is triggered by catastrophic events, economic instability, varying types of religious trauma, relationship missteps, and misplaced meaninglessness.

Meaninglessness results in what I refer to as *spiritual neurosis*, the type of depression that emanates from a hyper-exuberant interpretation of who someone is supposed to be because of who they understand God to be. Drawing from a warped understanding of being intentionally disadvantaged by a supreme mover and wishing to be at spiritual peace with oneself, spiritual neurosis features severe anxiety and depression, with presentations of inner turmoil about whether God is happy with "me" or whether "I am lost." By comparing themselves to God and feeling enormously inadequate, humans lacerate themselves and resort to spiritual isolation until there is, if it ever comes, a sense of earned piety that reflects what they believe has been obtained in obscurity and is now ready to be publicly displayed.

Amazingly, my observation with some clients treated for those types of clinical issues with religious features, recommendations to serve at a religious institution or to be charitable in other ways helps them develop a stronger sense of self-worthiness and spiritual maturity, even if they know they have not become God. But just to become aware of their vulnerability to anxiety, fear, depression, and other delusional features, clients with exposure to religious thought tend to respond differently to a more balanced view of God.

The desire for spiritual perfection cannot be underestimated as a significant trigger for spiritual failure or fanaticism. Caution is given here to those who have a balanced desire for spiritual maturity to avoid the abandonment their genuine spiritual motivations because others around them are experiencing spiritual failures or being religiously fanatical. Religious imbalance can motivate fanaticism, which can further fuel acts of antisocial behaviors, if left unchecked.

Fear *of* God must be differentiated from fear *for* God—being afraid of versus having respect for God. Although the expression "fear of God" is much used to refer to both "phobia of God" and "respect for God," more often than not, it presents a negative picture of who God is and His insatiable appetite for power, control, and universal dominance at all costs. We should stop anthropomorphizing God's behavior by giving it human qualities, such as consternation, which suggests that out of fear of disloyalty to His authoritarian government, humanity must be kept in check. Instead, we should search for scriptural processes that are shared across time and experiences to speak to who God is and His understanding of human emotions.

Fear in Biblical Language

Have you ever been so petrified from any encounter with a surprising, unusual, or threatening entity or been in the presence of something so awesome or amazing, and you say something like, "My gut tells me something is not right here," or "I can feel it in my gut"? This is the purest "feeling" reflected in the meaning of the Hebrew word *yarah*. The Hebrews were a very emotional people, and in many cases, their words would describe a "feeling" rather than an "action."

Some ten Hebrew nouns and eight verbs that are regularly translated as "fear," "to fear," or "to be afraid," spring from the root *yr* (the noun being *yirah*). The New Testament employs, almost exclusively, the use of the noun and verb *phobos* and *phobeo* respectively—also consistently used by the Septuagint to translate the Hebrew *yirah* and *yarah*. Phobos is one of those important words of the New Testament that is frequently overlooked by many. It is a word that depicts humanity's relationship to God, their fellows, judgment, authority, death, and salvation. Phobos, compared to the Hebrew noun yirah, expresses the protracted state of terror or alarm. Someone possessed by phobos is thus in a state of alarm because they are struck with the awesomeness of something or someone.

There are two other words translated as "fear" in the New Testament: *deilia*, which denotes cowardice, and *eulabeia*, whose basic idea is reverence. Phobos is so neutral a word that it is used to express the ideas not only of its own root but also of deilia and eulabeia. This must be remembered in the application of the existing root idea. Acts 9:31 (AKJV) renders that the Palestinian Christians were "walking in the fear of the Lord." The interpretation here is that the Christians were living reverent lives. The relationship here is noteworthy. The literal meaning of the verb fear, written as *yarah* and translated as "feeling" in the biblical Hebrew, refers to a "flowing of the gut," which can be applied to "fear" or "reverence."

For example, the text, "the fear (yirah) of the Lord is the beginning of wisdom: and the knowledge of the holy is understanding" (Proverbs 9:10 KJV), fear is equated with the "knowledge of the Holy One."

The word fear in this verse is the noun yirah, which is derived from the verb yarah. A surface reflection of the verse suggests that if one is afraid of or in great awe of Yahweh, one will have wisdom. This, however, is a limited interpretation of the text and use of the Hebrew language.

Therefore, "the fear of the Lord," which emanates out of Yahweh's substance, quintessentially is His omniscient teachings and His perfect character. Further, from a Hebrew perspective, we understand that the beginning of wisdom (*Chokhmah*—the ability to distinguish between good and bad) is resultant of the acceptance of the proceeds (Yirah, the teachings (Torah), and character [ru'ahh]) from Yahweh. That type of intimate relationship with God is spiritually empowering, reassuring, satisfying, and stabilizing.

A truly successful life is founded on fear of God. Biblical wisdom literature clearly emphasizes that the fear of the Lord is the beginning of wisdom (Proverbs 9:10; 1:7; Psalm 111:10 AKJV) because to fear God is to know Him, and to know Him is to fear Him. This is the inescapable unity. This is the medium that motivates a relationship of praise and adoration to God.

> The one who fears the Lord will praise Him (Psalm 22:23; Revelation 14:7 KJV).

> The one who fears the Lord will not be in want (Psalm 34:9 KJV).

> Those will fear the Lord will experience the height and depth of His greatness (Psalm 103:11 KJV).

> The blessings of God to those who fear Him will be passed on to the children's children (Psalm 103:17 KJV).

> The one who fears the Lord will rest in peace and security (Psalm 112:7–8 KJV).

> The one who fears the Lord will be blessed to experience length of days (Proverbs 10:27; 19:23 KJV).

Perception of God

A perception of who God is exists in the hearts of all humankind. Troubling to many is their inability to scientifically define God or give a logical definition of who they understand God to be. The quest of locating God within a higher concept of beings supremely coordinated within the sphere of extraterrestrial existence has confounded religious and scientific minds. The fact that God defies the definitions of humankind renders it impossible to give an academically exhaustive description of who God is.

We would be mindful to avoid the limitations of human description that portray God in abstract forms when the scriptures present one who is intrinsically empathetic and enters into relations with His creation. If after fasting forty days and forty nights, Jesus was hungry (Matthew 4:2 NIV), if "Jesus wept" (John 11:35 NLT), and if Jesus, on a boat with some of His disciples, slept in the middle of a storm (Matthew 8:24 AKJV), then Matthew's account of His name being Emmanuel (God with us) (Matthew 1:23 AKJV) is quite appropriate to conclude that "we do not have a high priest incapable of sympathizing with our weaknesses, but one who has been tempted in every way just as we are, yet without sin.is touched with the feelings of our infirmities" (Hebrews 4:15 NET).

So, you want to walk with God, but you're afraid.

You're afraid because your heart contains an unwelcoming portrayal of God. That disturbing portrayal has resulted in literal phobia, resulting from those who claim to have known God. Many view God as a tyrannical Father who is overwhelmingly overbearing, unrealistic, dismissive of others' desires, preoccupied with service and self-exaltation, manipulative by intent, non-pleasure seeking, and gloomy faced. They see Him as a hard taskmaster, who "reaps where he has not sown" (Matthew 25:24 AKJV), who expects what's unrealistic "sell what you have and give to the poor" (Matthew 19:21 AKJV), has gender bias, is racially challenged and ethnically biased, and is a selectively available male.

God has character. But what is the character of God? Bible-believing people know that one approach to understanding God is to understand His character. Further, we are told that God is love and that Jesus Christ was His greatest manifestation of this love on earth. We know also that God is our Creator (Genesis 2:26 AKJV). We know that God is our sustainer (Matthew 6:33 AKJV), and He keeps His creation in its perfect clocklike function (Genesis 2:27, Exodus 20:8 AKJV). We also know that God is a lawgiver (Exodus 20:1–26 AKJV), and an organizer (Genesis 2:1–25 AKJV). Furthermore, we are taught that God is a judge and a ruler. Beyond this, we know that God is our Father who is intimately interested in our welfare. These things are all well-known to any serious Bible scholar. But beyond this what is the actual substance, the physical makeup of God?

Is this your perception of God? If not, what is it? What is your definition of God? Who do you understand God to be? We are told in Psalm 90:2 (AKJV) that God is everlasting. This word *everlasting* is humans' feeble attempt to describe a situation for which they have no concept. Where does everlasting begin—and where does it end? Is it like a great circle with no specific starting point to wander far enough and then return to the original point? Do you believe that God exists? Are you open to getting to know God?

In the Pauline epistle of Colossians 2:3 (AKJV), we are told that God possesses all knowledge. Here, we are attempting to understand a situation for which we have no concept as mortal beings. How can anyone have unlimited knowledge? What is the source of God's knowledge? Does God seek knowledge from celestial books? Since God is everlasting, it would be only wise to assume that His knowledge likewise has been everlasting and not derived from study. This is an intangible concept since all our knowledge is acquired or instinctive. Both of these methods are obviously unacceptable explanations for an everlasting, omniscient God. In a world where everything is linked to life and death, beginning and end, the word *everlasting* has no verifiable meaning. Where all is finite, anything that is infinite is beyond our comprehension.

Another unique characteristic of God is His ability to sustain all that He has created. John the revelator, in Revelation 19:6 (AKJV), articulated it this way:

> And I heard as it were the voice of a great multitude, and as the voice of many waters, and as the voice of mighty thunderings, saying, Alleluia: for the Lord God omnipotent reigneth.

The statement implies that God is all-powerful. Again, this is a concept that is impossible for us mortals to fully assimilate.

As simple as these statements may sound, but they contain the genesis of your journey into a great existence. One's spiritual journey is the quintessence of all existence. Wrapped in the heart of one's spiritual journey is their social existence, material acquisitions, and human relationships. Central to success in all of those areas of existence is the principle of stewardship, which reveals God's ownership of all things. God's ownership of all things gives unlimited authority and access to all things at all times and for all people. No one is exempted from the largesse of God's blessings:

> That ye may be the children of your Father which is in heaven: for he maketh his sun to rise on the evil and on the good, and sendeth rain on the just and on the unjust. (Matthew 5:45 AKJV)

Everyone has been given access to heaven's storehouse.

Understandably, the fear of God also produces fear of divine wrath and judgment in those who do not know him or who refuse to serve him. Rebellion, the prophet Samuel said to the rejected King Saul, is as the sin of witchcraft. So, uneasiness with God can cause one to cower in dread and terror in anticipation of His wrath.

Your walk with God has not grown because of your phobia. You have not been able to scientifically support his existence or prove his caring nature, such as in the loss of a loved one. If this is your experience, let me officially welcome you to the hall of fame for those who have lived their lives seeking to disprove God's existence, seeking to disregard what they have experienced, and seeking to silence the innate voice that speaks loudly to a higher powerful existence.

I was told a story at Sabbath school some decades ago that I still remember today. The story was about a man who wanted to experience God for himself. He had been told that God was everywhere, all-powerful and all-knowing. He had read of events when God came through for people who were hard-pressed and in difficult places. This man had just lost a loved one. Out of anger that God didn't save his loved one, he stormed out of the house, stretched his hands toward the heavens and said, "God if you are there, if you are listening, if you care, show me your power. He waited for something to happen, but nothing did. Again, he shouted, "God if you are there, if you are listening, if you care, show me your power." Again, he waited. Nothing happened. For the third time, in a louder voice, he again asked for a sign: "God if you are there, if you are listening, if you care, show me your power." And he waited. At that time, lightning struck, and the area around him lit up with spectacular brightness. Amazed and powerless, he knelt to the ground and thanked God for who He is, what He did, and for favoring his requests.

Have you been like that man? If yes, you should not beat up on yourself. The Bible is replete with accounts of other persons whose walk with God was punctuated with similar questions, until God satisfied their sincerity. Abraham negotiated with the angel for the salvation of his nephew Lot and family from Sodom and Gomorrah (Genesis 18:16–33 AKJV). Moses, in his reluctance to speak truth to political powers, pointed out to God his low self-esteem, speech impediment, and lack of assertiveness (Exodus 3:1–15 AKJV). Gideon (Judges 6:1–40 AKJV) challenged God's power, presence, and wisdom three times to authenticate his call to ministry. Three times, he asked for signs to ascertain the credibility, authority, and power of the visiting angel. Every time he asked, God gave him the assurance that he would be with him even in fearful times.

God welcomes your interests in His plan for your life. God is not offended when His sons and daughters reason with him. God invites us to do so. "Come now let us reason together (Isaiah 1:18 AKJV). Reasoning is not monotonous. On the contrary, it is engaging—with disagreements and reassurances at times. Recognize that in each of those instances, when God engaged His appointees, they were transfixed and transformed for other service. In every one of the examples cited, individuals were being called into an intercessory role for supplication on behalf of others. Further, they all presented fearful features symptomatic of unbelief and disbelief, but they were elevated to the level of believer when God melted their doubts and reassured their faith.

Franklin Bray knows something about appealing to God. On countless occasions, I have appealed to God for my family and for others. However, out of the plethora of experiences that stand out to me, this unique one has been riveted to my heart's wall of faith. I remember explicitly how embarrassing it was, yet it was firmly reassuring of God's immediacy in my life (talking about God being a present help in trouble).

In graduate school, there were phases of financial challenges. One day I was so dismally financially challenged that I left the Library Resource Center and was walking toward the post office, asking God for some gas money. I said to God, "You know I don't have money to put gas in the car.

When my wife and I leave classes tonight, we need to get home. Lord, I don't have any other source but You. Please give me some money."

By the time my "open-eyes" prayer was over, I heard a voice that was as loud as a shout. The voice said, "Look in the drain, Franklin."

I immediately said, "What am I looking in the drain for?"

The voice said, "Franklin, look in the drain."

Hesitantly, I looked into the drain and there was a dollar bill. I glanced around me and stepped into the partially watered drain to pick up the much-needed bill. Gas was ninety cents a gallon at the time. God provided again to strengthen my faith. I was reminded of what Jesus himself cautioned His disciples, about the quest of many to receive a sign in order that they may alleviate their fear.

Faith Is Needed on the Journey

The declaration of the charter text of the Bible must be made here:

> But without faith it is impossible to please him: for he that cometh to God must believe that he is, and that he is a rewarder of them that diligently seek him. By faith Noah, being warned of God of things not seen as yet, moved with fear, prepared an ark to the saving of his house; by the which he condemned the world, and became heir of the righteousness which is by faith. (Hebrews 11:6, 7 AKJV)

This is explosively motivational. Faith in God activates a relationship with Him and gives a good report of the one who believes and demonstrates faith. The demands of the journey require the development of faith in God. Not in anyone or anything experienced on your journey. This is not the same as having confidence in the weather reporter. The weather reporter can be seen and can be heard. The weather developments are verifiable, trackable, and sometimes predictable. It is not so when walking with God. His ways are past finding out. The premise to begin the journey with God is the same motivation needed to complete the journey. By faith, the dethroning of fear makes serving God possible.

Leaders Demand a Miraculous Sign

> One day the Pharisees and Sadducees came to test Jesus, demanding that he show them a miraculous sign from heaven to prove his authority. He replied, "You know the saying, 'Red sky at night means fair weather tomorrow; red sky in the morning means foul weather all day.' You know how to interpret the weather signs in the sky, but you don't know how to interpret the signs of the times! Only an evil, adulterous generation would demand a miraculous sign, but the only sign I will give them is the sign of the prophet Jonah." Then Jesus left them and went away. (Matthew 16:1–4 NLT)

In the early stages of our walk with God, God understands that we need some reassurance—and oftentimes, it comes by a strange measure of inner peace that we would never have had before. In that time, we know without a doubt that God is alive and has showed up in our hearts. The peace that surpasses all understanding. When you need to know more about God, he understands that and will not leave you comfortless.

He also gives us that reassurance when we are unsure of what next steps to take. God will open doors and close them, and the Holy Spirit who came to comfort us will tell us what we need to know. It may take something a little more obvious for some of us, but the Lord gives us signs to affirm our walk and say, "Yes, this is the path I want you to walk, this is what I have planned for you."

We shouldn't ask for the undeniable promises that He has already given. It is significant to ask certain questions: "Does God love me?" Of course, He gave up the very best heaven had to offer while we were yet sinners" John 3:16 (AKJV). "Will God provide for me?" He promised that He will (Matthew 6:33 AKJV). "Will He save me?" He gave His Son so that all may have eternal life. "Am I righteous?" If any man be in Christ, he is a new creation (2 Corinthians 5:17 AKJV). He has proven that He loves us all. God did so through his son who came to die for us so that we may all, through redemption from the penalty of sin, become His children.

Therefore, fear of God must be differentiated from fear for God. Fear of God is a result of our understanding of who God is, His interest in our lives, and the availability of His presence for our nurturance. Fear for God is an acceptance of who God is and our willingness to provide Him with worship in all that we are and all that we do. Phobia for God does not exist in the relationship of one who knows God.

ASSESSMENT QUESTIONS

What is my perception of God?

_____

_____

Do I live in fear of God or in fear for God?

_____

_____

What about God motivates me to live in fear of Him?

_____

_____

What experiences have I had that confirm the need to live in fear for God?

_____

_____

How has living in fear of God benefited my walk with Him?

_____

_____

Have I ever tried negotiating with God? What was that moment like?

_____

_____

For the next seven days, ask God to plant in your heart the desire to know Him as a friend. Enjoy the relationship as it flourishes. Note the growth.

_____

_____

No man loves the man whom he fears

- Aristotle

CHAPTER 2

Fear: The Emotion

To fear is to express humanity. Humanity is flawed. Fear finds humanity attractive. We respond so frequently and immeasurably to its mating calls that we are hopeless to its seductive, vulnerable, and emotionally indiscriminate voice. Would you agree? Well, I am. So embedded in me is that reality that I am very concerned about the plight of those who have a limited understanding of fear.

Many have dismissed fear as a mere physiological phantom, a spiritual necessity, a psychological misnomer, a negative emotion, or a personality flaw with minimal, if any, consequential impact. I understand the difficulty in making that assumption, and I understand it to be the consequence of downplaying the nature of fear and the dreadful reality that comes with its occupation. You see, many have failed to accept that fear, as an emotion, is always triggered by the conclusion that something negative is impacting me—and I need to do everything possible to stop engaging whatever that is stimulating the negativity or danger, which takes the body into a defensive mode for some action or another.

A study of the word fear reveals that it is the translation of the ancient Greek word *Φόβος*, Phobos, from which we get the word *phobia*. In Greek mythology, Phobos is the god of fear. He is the son of Ares (the god of war) and Aphrodite (the goddess of love). Phobos was known to be an attendant of his father alongside some of his siblings. In classical Greek literature, he was considered to be the personification of fear, and he does not appear as a character in myths.

In modern language, fear is used in the context of phobia, which is the overwhelming and debilitating fear of a person, place, situation, feeling, animal, situation, or object. Phobias are generally more pronounced than fears. They develop when a person has an exaggerated or unrealistic sense of danger about a situation or object. That irrationality, if it becomes very severe, will motivate people to organize their lives around avoiding the thing that's causing them anxiety. Their normal functioning is restricted, which results in much distress.

To experience fear is normal and natural to all species, including *Homo sapiens*. It is very important that you accept this position in order to move to the next level of debunking the lie that only ungodly, evil, rebellious, or psychologically distressed individuals experience fear. So, let's accept that fear is a normal reality that impacts the lives of all human beings and that some moments of fear are unconscious.

Fear is often confused with anxiety. However, fear and anxiety are not the same experiences. Although the terminologies are used interchangeably in common parlance, they remain conceptually and physiologically distinct. Fear is experienced when trying to avoid or escape aversive stimuli. That intense emotion is aroused by the detection of a clearly identifiable and specific threat, which involves an immediate alarm reaction that mobilizes the organism by triggering a set of physiological changes. These include rapid heartbeat, redirection of blood flow away from the periphery and toward the gut, tensing of the muscles, and a general mobilization of the organism to take some type of action. When we face a threat, the endocrine system releases glucocorticoids and other hormones, which turn up the systems we need to protect ourselves and turn down the signals that are not immediately useful for survival.

Fear negatively impacts our physical health. Living under constant threat has inconceivable health consequences and should never be minimized. Epidemiological researchers have for decades linked high stress levels to psycho-neuro-immunological issues, a weakened immune system, increased cardiovascular damage, gastrointestinal problems such as ulcers and irritable bowel syndrome, and decreased fertility.

Fear is known to cause impairment in the formation of long-term memories and damage to certain parts of the brain, including the hippocampus. When this happens, the brain is less able to regulate fear, which can leave a person anxious most of the time. Someone who lives with constant or chronic fear sees the world as a gloomy place, and that image is confirmed by the difficulty in forming pleasant memories. Other symptoms include fatigue, an increased likelihood of osteoporosis, type 2 diabetes, exacerbated clinical depression, accelerated aging, and even premature death.

Fear impedes the management of emotions. The disruption is noteworthy because it impacts the processes in our brains that allow us to read nonverbal cues, regulate emotions, reflect before acting, act ethically, and decipher information. Where the management of emotions has been compromised, thought processes and decision-making capacities are constricted, which leaves us susceptible to intense emotions and impulsive reactions. The ability to act appropriately is weakened, leaving us vulnerable to external factors.

Fear must be managed because of possible genetic predispositions generated by exposure to traumatic events. Although scientific research is still evolving about genetically inherited fear and anxiety, some researchers have argued,

> **What we should not fear is everything that exists. What we should embrace is everything that will serve to better our lives and the lives of others.**

for example, that children and grandchildren of Holocaust survivors stand a higher risk for chronic fear, depression, post-traumatic stress, and anxiety than contemporaries who had not been similar experiences. This is possible because of the impact of traumatic events on the lives of their ancestors.

Further research has indicated that descendants of survivors of other massive traumas, especially slavery and attempted genocide, often report symptoms that are similar to those experienced by the people who endured the traumas themselves. The existence of inherited grief, fear, and anxiety among Native Americans, African Americans, and other marginalized cultural groups suggest inherited trauma, which compounds the systemic realities of racial discrimination and brutalities of this present age.

Anxiety, on the other hand, is characterized by apprehension and somatic symptoms of tension when there is the anticipation of some level of danger, disappointment, or disaster. The anticipation mobilizes physiological responses that include body tension, heavy breathing, and rapid heartbeat.

Even if we were to wish, we cannot undo what appear to be deeply ingrained patterns of psychological responses to existing or potential societal threats. The first, most important, step is to recognize and accept that our experiences are real and have real effects on our behavior and our health, regardless of whether those perceptions are grounded in facts that are supported by science.

As a matter of fact, unknown to us, we may unconsciously display or express fear about environmental issues. We experience frustrations because of societal policies and our own idiosyncrasies. The less we trust the people who are supposed to protect us—or the people, governments, or corporate institutions exposing us to perceived dangerous situations—the more afraid we will be. The more we trust, the less fear we feel.

The Word of God warns against the infiltration and occupation of fear in our lives. I reintroduce here what is going to be a favorite staple in this text. So, choose your servings. It is found in the menu from the apostle Paul:

> For God has not given us a spirit of fear and timidity, but
> of power, love, and self-discipline. (2 Timothy 1:7 NLT)

For the Spirit God gave us does not make us timid, but gives us power, love and self-discipline. (2 Timothy 1:7 NIV)

For God did not give us a spirit of cowardice, but rather a spirit of power and of love and of self-discipline. (2 Timothy 1:7 NRSV)

Regardless of the amount you choose to serve yourself or the amount you preferred to have been plated for you, the serving is unequivocally explicit. God does not delight in timidity and did not give it to us. Fear, as an emotion, does not have to be scheduled in order to be experienced. It is not a degeneration of the personality or a mental illness. Fearfulness, timidity, and cowardice are environmentally learned and nurtured. It is a compromise of the willpower, consciously or unconsciously, to accommodate self-preservation when it is perceived or is justifiably under attack.

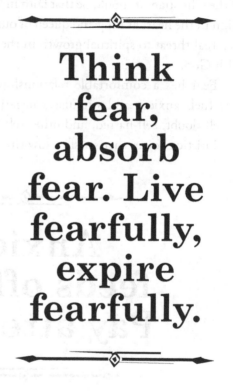

Think fear, absorb fear. Live fearfully, expire fearfully.

Fear can be temporary or prolonged. As a temporary experience, the emotion can usually be replaced with another emotion that favors the individual or reaffirms confidence in the environment that conducted the feeling of fear to the body. As a physiological response, fear is linked to other body emotions. Fear can trigger anxiety, and anxiety can intensify fear. However, a person who marinates fearful thoughts will motivate fearful behaviors in themselves and others over whom they have influence, which is another solid reason to select your friends from the infinite number of persons you come across daily.

Phobos is also used in a negative sense in Romans 13:3 (AKJV); the apostle Paul characterized it as the emotion of the ungodly. He expressed the connection that a religion based on legalism reduces a man to a slave, and the dominant emotion of a slave is Phobos (Romans 8:15 AKJV). A religion dominated by law is dominated by fear and is therefore inadequate since the Christian religion is one of love. Love is the spiritual compulsion of the Christian. It should be that faith in God recognizes fear's intention to reign in the heart as king and queen of our lives. It is rightfully understood as a real threat to spiritual growth in the hearts of all who desire to walk with God.

Fear has a comfortable relationship with anxiety. As an emotion, fear fuels anxiety and stimulates negative behavior. It limits its victim to self-doubt, self-hatred, and other self-destructive behaviors, including pessimistic choices that satisfy a low threshold of comfort.

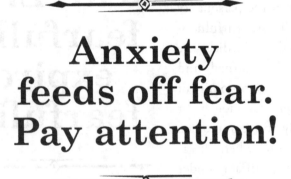

Anxiety feeds off fear. Pay attention!

Heidi was an excellent biology student in high school and in her undergraduate program. Her career choice was medicine. As befits a diligent and rigorous academic, Heidi spent much time gathering information about the universities that would provide her with the maximum advantage of realizing her dream. Acceptance letters with generous financial packages came from three outstanding universities.

There was much jubilation when the packages were first received. As time progressed and an acceptance decision was drawing closer, Heidi began expressing anxiety about the possibility of not doing well in medical school. She was deeply perturbed because she did not see the possible source of financial support since both of her parents were unemployed.

Heidi began spending much time in isolation, doubting her future and raising question after question about her decision to attend medical school. Her dream became less attractive to her and rejecting all three offers was becoming more palatable to her than anything else. One week before the deadline for the acceptance of an offer, Heidi was hospitalized for panic attacks. She was having unusual stomach pains and lost interests in her grooming. Heidi's hospitalization assessment revealed that her fear of not having all the funding for medical school raised anxiety about her future, and the need to decide felt like the walls were rapidly closing in on her. After release from hospitalization, Heidi submitted her acceptance letter to the first school of her choice. The days following, Heidi began a journey through psychotherapy as she prepared for the challenges of medical school.

Heidi is not the only person who has experienced panic attacks. None of us is immune to that reality. The difference is in the acceptance of our humanity, our frailty, our vulnerabilities, our spirituality, and the presence or lack of dogged determination to fight weaknesses in ourselves and in our environments.

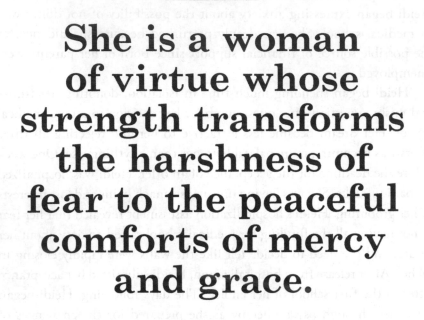

She is a woman of virtue whose strength transforms the harshness of fear to the peaceful comforts of mercy and grace.

As a fear-defeating commandment, we have the following spiritual principle to guide us on the journey through the hills of anxiety and despair:

> Do not be anxious about anything, but in every situation,
> by prayer and petition, with thanksgiving, present your
> requests to God. And the peace of God, which transcends
> all understanding, will guard your hearts and your minds
> in Christ Jesus. (Philippians 4:6–7 NIV)

Bear in mind that there are times when a memory may result in the reemergence of fear in your body. You may even feel like you are experiencing déjà vu in a traumatic way. Emotional memory plays a significant role here. This can happen even if you are in the comfort of trusted friends or a familiar place. Unexplained sweating or reactions may be triggered by the powerful memory of a negative experience. You may experience a panic attack because you have fed your memory with so much fear that it is easier to respond with fear to an unfamiliar or uncomfortable situation than with assertiveness and mature boldness.

Do not live in fear of fear; instead, recognize it as an element that is manipulatable by you. Society already has so much that can stimulate fear in our lives. Walking through certain places, hearing emergency sirens, reading billboards or graffiti on broken-down walls, or smelling something putrid may be enough to emotionally charge you with fear. You don't need to compound those unwanted experiences.

Learn to sufficiently challenge your memory. Learn to constantly challenge your memory. By so doing, negative reminders will become less and less your favorite reminders. However, if they do, you will have developed sufficient skills to weaken their power over your life. This will not come from wishing, reading, or even praying. It comes from diligent practice. If you desire victory over fear, it is time to execute all of the principles you have discovered.

> **He is a man of courage who does not run away, but remains at his post and fights against the enemy.**
>
> —Socrates

Live with as little of that emotional charge as possible. Live boldly. Live maturely. Live assertively. Live knowledgeably. Live with confidence. Live with inspiration. Live without prejudice for race, color, or religion. Live to be a blessing to all people. Live to leave the much-needed legacy that God favors boldness over timidity and that provision has been made to give everyone victory over cowardice in behavior and in character. Where there is dispute over your management skills or capacity to do so, find trusted help. Do not give in to the domineering character of fear.

Fear is the seed of destruction and not the opportunity to rise higher. Fear is at the heart of all destruction. We all need to remember that throughout our spiritual sojourn. What we should not fear is everything that exists to us or to others. What we should embrace is everything that will serve to better our lives and the lives of others. Fear thrives on the disposition to feel incapacitated. Fear occupies the soul where spirituality is wanting. The more uncertain we are, the more we seek to protect ourselves with precaution and fear. If all life's answers are unavailable, as with scientific discoveries today, our concern will be higher. However, even if the answers we seek are available, if they are difficult to understand, for example, like the science of Pfizer-BioNTech, Moderna, AstraZeneca COVID-19 vaccination, or is abysmally explained, people are left uncertain and, as a result, more afraid.

Knowledge, by itself, does not necessarily stop fear's occupation of the soul. Before you spend too much time misinterpreting, let me explain. The application of knowledge reduces fear's grip on our lives. Bear in mind that fear disenfranchises and spreads unbelief. This is evident in all areas of our lives, including past, present, and potentially future relationships. Socially, fear raises the concern of apprehension: "It's too good to be true." Psychologically, fear stimulates neurotic and delusion behaviors: "I am being watched or spied on." Spiritually, its intent is to shatter any possibility of positive development and in this case, question the intention of the Creator in creating humankind.

Here again, I raise the provision God made against fear. He gave us a spirit of love, power, and self-discipline. The fundamental reason for God not giving us a spirit of fear is because we would not be free to exercise and develop the potential with which we were created. We would not have been able to know Him, develop a relationship with Him, or emotionally interact with other beings. We would be mere automatons without the capacity to operate beyond our programming. Happily, this is not the case! We are free moral agents with the capacity to discover, build, bond, and procreate.

If fear was allowed to dominate our lives, we would be destroying the very things that we need for healthy living, comfort, and safety. For example, a risk that kills us in a horrifying way evokes more fear than one that kills more benignly (vehicular accident versus cancer, being eaten alive by a shark or dying of heart disease). Heart problems are prevalent (fear, anxiety, anger, and depression as major contributors) and far more likely to kill us, but a dreadful death often provokes more fear.

Fear immobilizes and targets the soul of its unsuspecting victims. It is very subtle yet decisively uncompromising in its attacks. Its aim is to dominate. In order for domination to be effective, its potential victims are unsuspecting, distracted, or too weak to put up a defense. Fortunately, many have survived the vicious attacks of fear and live with the scars to tell their stories. No one can claim not having been attacked and having survived. One who is not able to admit having been fearful is deficient in character. Hence, the greatest fear of humankind is the fear of fear.

Courage is knowing what not to fear.

—Plato

The relationship between physiological and spiritual fear should not be underestimated. The viciousness of the physical will show up on the spiritual journey if the genesis of fear is highlighted:

> For God has not given us a spirit of fear and timidity, but
> of power, love, and self-discipline. (2 Timothy 1:7 NLT)

ASSESSMENT QUESTIONS

What do I fear?

_____

_____

Does my experience with disappointment motivate fear in me?

_____

_____

How much do I excuse the presence of fear in my life?

_____

_____

Am I prepared to assess the impact of my memories on my life?

_____

_____

Am I anxious about my future? Am I afraid that I'm anxious?

_____

_____

Do I feel inadequate with myself because of others' perceptions of me?

_____

_____

What specific memories stirs a panicky feeling in me?

_____

_____

Deficient in character is the one who is unwilling to admit having been fearful.

—Plato

Fear the seed of destruction, not the opportunity to challenge yourself and rise higher.

CHAPTER 3

Fear: The Behavior

Fear motivates irreverence for God.

I attended a church service where the young youth pastor passionately prayed, thanked God for His mercies, and requested favor for the prosperity of the church, for the strengthening of the youth, and for youth-development opportunities. He ended by saying, "Talk to you later, buddy. Amen!"

Let me immediately share with you my reason for highlighting that illustration in this chapter. I am a second-generation Seventh-day Adventist Christian believer, an ordained minister of religion, and a firm believer in supplicatory prayer. I believe in having a friendship with God that is personal and charged. However, I was shell-shocked. My jaw dropped. I was shocked to have heard for the first time in my lifetime, someone ending a prayer the way the young youth pastor did.

I was religiously surprised, theologically challenged, and deeply spiritually troubled because I heard extremes in the statement after such a passionate prayer. From that theologically challenged, spiritually troubled prayer, I received the picture of a bosom relationship that requires little or no formality in worship, a relationship that is being taken for granted, and a relationship that lacks depth and is purely casual. In no way will I spend time dissecting my assumption or interpretation of the prayer or motivation of the youth pastor to pray such a prayer. I am, however, concerned that extremes in our relationships with God can be spiritually defeating. We can, with our actions and our words, be confirming the proverb "familiarity breeds contempt." That's a dangerous place to be relationally and spiritually.

Fear of God shows in overcompensation in religious rituals. The irrational overextension of oneself to indicate to others that "I am spiritual" is often confused with "I am exerting my energies, time, and resources because I love God. Therefore, I will do everything possible to share his love with all who need to know Him." I can appreciate the behavior that says, "I love the Lord, and there is nothing that is too hard for me to do for His cause."

Allow me to be clear. I stand in jubilation with the breaking of every alabaster box to honor the Lord with a heartfelt offering of gratitude for His grace and mercies. I am not pointing this out as overcompensation. Simply put, seeking to gain God's favor—or to appease His wrath by presenting His cause with expensive gifts when the heart is not with the cause—is futile and does not contribute to spiritual growth. Many are caught in that religious misnomer. They give much of their time and resources as a way to move God into loving them. They fear that if they

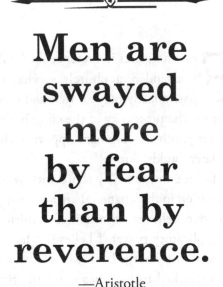

Men are swayed more by fear than by reverence.

—Aristotle

don't do so, they will be visited with God's undiluted wrath. So, the extremes remain evident: much casualness or much conservatism. Both are spiritually defeating.

Respect for God requires sincerity, transparency, contrition, and humility. Those dispositions reflect one's understanding of God's majesty and the limitations of humankind. When one approaches a power of significance, it requires respect for the position and a lack of manipulation for the purpose of receiving favor from that power. Fear, being afraid of, may not necessarily be absent, but it should be acknowledged as a hindrance to providing sincere service. Respect for God should not be translated to such casual behavior as to demonstrate a lack of honor for who God is. Worship of God cannot be void of sincerity. Either extreme is fatal, indicating a dearth of openness in the relationship with God. The legalists are afraid they will fall out of covenantal walk with God and stir His wrath. The liberals, on the other hand, feel that because they have a covenant with God, what they do will be interpreted in the spirit of the relationship.

We must never become too casual and give up respect for God. We must realize when we address our heavenly Father that He is Abba, position of Daddy, but never forget that He is also El Shaddai, the Almighty God. Hence the spiritual principle of reverencing (respecting, honoring) God. This is why we are required to possess the fear of God. It is not a fear of God hurting us; it is the fear of stepping out of favor with Him and grieving the relationship. At this point, you may say, "But I'm in Christ; nothing can hurt our relationship." That stance reflects a person who has a doctrinal arrangement and not a relationship. Maybe we need to rethink and realize nothing can hurt our convictions, except disrespect and unfaithfulness to God, in our relationship with Him.

Fear can alter the depth and significance of your relationship with God. Fear of who God is and what God can do may be so intimidating to you that staying away from Him may be seen as the best alternative. The reason is simple. The relationship is contractual and not one of worship. Relating to God on a contractual basis always results in legalism or casualness. Legalism because of fear, and casualness because of oversimplicity and position differentiation. Relationship does not equate sameness. The legalist is afraid that breaking a covenant with God will result in Him unleashing His wrath. The liberal feels that because "I have a covenant with God, the wrong that I do does not matter. God will continue to regard and honor me as His child." The perception a person has about God will significantly influence what they do and what they don't do.

My experience has proven that religious dogma has instilled much fear in the hearts of those who should be serving God happily. Fear of eternal damnation is major. Fear of disappointing parents is among a plethora of reasons why many children get baptized and become members of Protestant churches. Don't get me wrong. Many children become members of the body of Christ because of their love for Him, but being afraid of punishment is the motivation of many. The same can be said for many Christians who struggle with sexual sins, including homosexual practices and other illicit activities such as illegal drug dealing (much more will be said about this type of attitude in another chapter).

Fear as a behavior is a direct reflection of fear as an emotion. I refer to them as biological siblings that contend for attention at the weirdest times. Fear as a phobia motivates a movement away from the very thing needed to stir a productive relationship in your walk with God and in your relationship with others. The extremes exist. There are some who reverence God and worship Him with humility, others are afraid of him, and some take Him casually and practice a non-reverential approach to him.

The negative characterization of fear cannot be overlooked in the appreciation of healthy fear. In Romans 13:3 (AKJV), *phobos* is used in a bad sense. The apostle Paul characterized it as the emotion of the ungodly. He identified the difference between a walk with God based on liberty and love and a walk that is contrived of legalism. Phobos (cowardice) of God expresses a religion based on legalism, which reduces a man to a slave, and the dominant emotion of a slave is service out of *phobos* (Romans 8:15 AKJV). A religion dominated by law is dominated by fear and is therefore inadequate since the Christian religion is one of love.

The greatest fear of humankind is the fear of fear.

Phobia of God motivates a legalistic response to God and fuels fanaticism. The extremes, though they appear convincingly beneficial to your spiritual journey, will result in an emptiness that will spiral down to depression and feelings of rejection.

Fear of God is linked to increased depression, fear of rejection, heightened anxiety, fear of never being good enough for God, fear your prayers won't be answered because you believe the value of your prayers is linked to your relationship with God and how good you are now and not how good you have been in the past. You will be motivated to apply scripture verses such as Proverbs 28:9 (NIV): "If anyone turns a deaf ear to my instruction, even their prayers are detestable." I am heartened to know that the scriptures also readily provide a response to those of us who may question God's willingness to hear and to answer our prayers.

> For the scripture saith, "Whosoever believeth on him shall not be ashamed. For there is no difference between the Jew and the Greek: for the same Lord over all is rich unto all that call upon him. For whosoever shall call upon the name of the Lord shall be saved." (Romans 10:11–13 KJV)

You may not have the faith of any of the venerated dead patriarchs of the scriptures, but you can surely pray like the musician, adulterer, murderer, bloodthirsty avenger, permissive parent, and king, David:

> Hear my cry, O God; attend unto my prayer. From the end of the earth will I cry unto thee, when my heart is overwhelmed: lead me to the rock that is higher than I. (Psalm 61:1, 2 KJV)

Deceptively, the adversary would have you believe that there is conditionality to having your prayers heard and having a rejuvenated life. The enemy is doing an excellent job at that. I would go further to say that his emphasis on knowing that you are perfect before thinking of approaching God, has gained traction in too many lives. The more he can convince persons like you and me to call on God only when we believe that we have justifiable reasons to feel good about ourselves, the more we are in great danger of not walking with God. You see, it's already a challenge to exercise faith in someone you have never seen but are motivated to believe because of how convincing the evidence is around you. Don't allow the enemy of all happiness to bamboozle out of our lives the foundation of our joy. Quit focusing on how "not good enough" you are and accept how willing God is to accept you despite all the flaws that come with just being human.

Living in fear of God leads to unrealistic covenants and a nonproductive existence. I grew up in a predominantly Roman Catholic community and have strong memories of the rituals and songs that I experienced in my childhood. A song by Edmund Vaughan is riveted in my head:

> God of mercy and compassion
> Look with pity upon me,
> Father, let me call thee father
> Tis thy child returns to thee
>
> Jesus Lord, I ask for mercy
> Let me not implore in vain,
> All my sins I now detest them,
> Never will I sin again.

I did not understand the depth of those statements then, but I believed them and sought to apply them in my personal life and compel them in the lives of many childhood friends. Some have passed, and many others are no longer part of the church organization. I strongly believed the emphasis was incorrect then as it is now in many Christian circles, where the desire for utopia motivates an unrealistic assumption of perfection, deluding aspirants of what is not humanly attainable. I have forgiven myself for whatever influence I may have had in them absorbing the implicit perfection that comes with confession of sins. Another example of this heightened fear is the compulsion for a long list of New Year's resolutions to appease the wrath of God for persons not caring for themselves, their neighbors and their children, not achieving their goals, and being inconsistent in their spiritual lives and relationships.

Those who are afraid to use their God-given gifts will blame God for not activating the motivation to use those gifts. They will blame God for not having been available to them, for not providing instructions on how, why, and where to do what they need to do. Consequently, ambition is stifled, potential stays dormant, hope dissipates, morale is low, the hope for legacy fades, and the blame game begins.

The sad notion in all of this is that a sign is posted about God that is woefully untrue. The fearful behavior says, "It cannot be done." The one who walks in the fear of God (majestical power of God) recognizes fear but understands that "with God, all things are possible" (Matthew 19:26 AKJV).

You should apply some behaviors to your fears. Demonstrate your understanding of fearlessness. Fear, as a behavior, will physically immobilize you, socially isolate you, psychologically defeat you, economically deprive you, and spiritually enslave you.

Firstly, manage what your mind believes about fear. Know that a fearful behavior is reflective of a mind that feeds on fear. Fear, as a behavior, distracts the most ambitious individual, slows down the fastest athlete, weakens the strongest body, disturbs the best mood, and heightens frustrations in the unsuspecting. Act now to benefit or experience a disparaging existence driven by fear.

Secondly, stand up to your fears. When you stand up to your fears, you are taking responsibility for your thoughts and your behaviors. By your actions, you are making the bold statement that I will develop me, and I will strengthen me through the development of my character. Character is destiny. Therefore, no pain should be spared in the process of developing the foundation of your legacy. God is not against you, and He is not working against His plan for you.

Thirdly, step into your fears. They are not bigger than God. God is not intimidated by what evil promotes. Boldly step into your fears. Boldness requires courage. Courage requires character. Virtuous character requires intentionality, and negative character does not. Therefore, you should not risk not having what you need for your journey because you are afraid. When you deliberately step into your fears, you will experience phenomenal transformations and positively impact those around you. You will transcend your expectations of yourself, those imposed limitations, and you will shatter the ceiling ceremoniously gifted to you by others.

Fourthly, prepare to exterminate your fear. Remember it is contagious. Fear as a behavioral response stimulates greater levels of fear and dissipates energy levels to a depressing low. Remember that. It either motivates you toward or away from the promise. It must be rightly appropriated. God does not need us to be afraid of Him. He wants us to embrace Him. Our behaviors will limit what we know we should have—even when the Word of God has already told us that we should have them:

> For the Lord God is a sun and shield: the Lord will give grace and glory: no good thing will he withhold from them that walk uprightly. No good gift will He withhold from them that walketh uprightly. (Psalm 84:11 KJV)

> So if you sinful people know how to give good gifts to your children, how much more will your heavenly Father give good gifts to those who ask him. (Matthew 7:11 NLT)

Never befriend fear. It will compel you to believe your doubts. It will sap you of the much-needed energy to move forward and convince you to accept the words of others (family, friends, and parishioners) as the viable direction for your life. I am in no

Fear is at the heart of all destruction.

way implying the rejection of discussion over matters that require the input of necessary people, but even when dialoguing is imperative, you need to have a conviction about your conviction. Your conviction, your dream, should speak to you louder than everyone else. It would be a blessing if others believe it and propel you along your much-anticipated path. But if not, own the rejection and rally yourself up the mountain of phenomenal success. It's your dream! Not mine! You have to take possession of it. You have to own it.

Fear, disguised as supportive friends, will lurk around for as long as you allow it. As a behavioral response, fear results in avoiding interactions with a confrontational stimulus, unconsciously eliciting confusion from self and others. To act fearful is an indication of your understanding of the perceived threat. To live fearfully is a profound statement that you are in a constant state of fear and lack the fortitude to move forward.

When there is something you want to achieve or do, it is self-defeating to lose your nerve while trying to convince other people about what you know you have to do. You know what you have to do. So, go ahead and get it done. It's yours to get done! It's your journey! With God on your side, get it done!

> "Great is Thy faithfulness," O God my Father,
> There is no shadow of turning with Thee;
> Thou changest not, Thy compassions, they fail not
> As Thou hast been Thou forever wilt be.
>
> "Great is Thy faithfulness!" "Great is Thy faithfulness!"
> Morning by morning new mercies I see;
> All I have needed Thy hand hath provided—
> "Great is Thy faithfulness," Lord, unto me!
>
> Summer and winter, and springtime and harvest,
> Sun, moon and stars in their courses above,
> Join with all nature in manifold witness
> To Thy great faithfulness, mercy and love.
>
> Pardon for sin and a peace that endureth,
> Thine own dear presence to cheer and to guide;
> Strength for today and bright hope for tomorrow,
> Blessings all mine, with ten thousand beside![1]

Sadly, some are always fearing and borrowing trouble. Every day they are surrounded by the tokens of God's love, every day they are enjoying the bounties of his providence; but they overlook these present blessings.

---

[1] Author: Thomas O. Chisholm, Music by William M. Runyan (c) 1923, Ren. 1951 Hope Publishing Co., Carol Stream, IL 60188 (Entered Public Domain in 2019).

Their minds are continually dwelling upon something disagreeable which they fear may come: or some difficulty may really exist, which, though small, blinds their eyes to the many things which demand gratitude. The difficulties which they encounter, instead of driving them to God, the only source of help, separate them from him, because of their awaken unrest and repining.

ASSESSMENT QUESTIONS

What reason(s) do I have to fear God?

_____

_____

Have I ever considered how fear has kept me from achieving my goals?

_____

_____

What is my usual reaction when I am confronted about my fearful disposition?

_____

_____

How much time do I spend worrying about the control fear has over my life?
Compare that to the amount of time I've invested in dismantling fear's grip on my life.

_____

_____

Am I trying to be good enough so that I won't have to worry about my imperfections?
(Try counting your imperfections and record how you feel after having done so).

_____

_____

Take a blank piece of paper and itemize the last risks you took that didn't have a possible failing point. On that same sheet of paper, itemize all that you have accomplished even when you saw fear lurking in the background. How do you feel about your efforts in taking risks and in succeeding?

_____

_____

How would I feel if I were to take time today to record all the doubts I have about my life?

_____

_____

CHAPTER 4

Fear of Spiritual Contamination

---◆---

Attitude is the sole determinant to establish or cancel all victories.

---◆---

I have been shown that the fear of spiritual contamination has kept Christians from being known as living epistles of the Gospel they preach. (This is what the Holy Spirit has ministered to me). The Bible is replete with references advocating abstinence from behaviors and lifestyles that can lead to spiritual contamination. None comes to the fore more strongly than 2 John 2:15–17 (KJV):

> Love not the world, neither the things that are in the world. If any man love the world, the love of the Father is not in him. For all that is in the world, the lust of the

flesh, and the lust of the eyes, and the pride of life, is not of the Father, but is of the world. And the world passeth away, and the lust thereof: but he that doeth the will of God abideth for ever.

A perfunctory view of the text immediately presents a dark hatred for the world——if not a divine permission to be defiantly oppositional to the world and its structures. The idea of isolationism comes to mind: how the avoidance of world interaction is fundamentally essential as part of ensuring a flawless Christian existence.

Needless to say, the principle taught in the text is often misconstrued by many devout Christians, aspirants, and those seeking to validate their reasons for the rejection of Christianity. A thorough analysis of the text will indicate the mandate to avoid the adoption of beliefs, behaviors, and lifestyle practices that will support and establish the wrongful practices of the unbelieving. The emphasis is placed on spiritual authenticity, spiritual identity, spiritual purity, and spiritual loyalty—and not on physical distancing for the fear of spiritual contamination.

Blessed is the one who does not walk in step with the wicked or stand in the way that sinners take or sit in the company of mockers, but whose delight is in the law of the Lord, and who meditates on his law day and night. That person is like a tree planted by streams of water, which yields its fruit in season and whose leaf does not wither— whatever they do prospers. (Psalm 1 NIV)

And what agreement hath the temple of God with idols? for ye are the temple of the living God; as God hath said, I will dwell in them, and walk in them; and I will be their God, and they shall be my people. Wherefore come out from among them, and be ye separate, saith the Lord, and touch not the unclean thing; and I will receive you, and will be a Father unto you, and ye shall be my sons and daughters, saith the Lord Almighty. (Corinthians 6:16–18 AKJV)

Abstain from every form of evil. (Thessalonians 5:22 NRSV)

Dear friends, I urge you, as foreigners and exiles, to abstain from sinful desires, which wage war against your soul. (Peter 2:11 NIV)

Many adherents of the Bible are confused about the levels of interaction they should have with nonbelievers. Consequently, they segregate themselves from those who are different from them, especially in race, economics, and faith. On one hand are those Christians who are genuinely afraid that their virtues will get corrupted; they sincerely believe that segregating from others outside of their comfortable spiritual communities will benefit their spiritual development. On the other hand, there are those who have gotten so assimilated with the world that they have lost their virtues, their identities, and their authenticity; they are now unrecognizable in the world. The former has been one of the greatest misconceptions of Christianity and the casting of a major shadow over the welcoming Gospel of Jesus Christ. The latter is a total misconception of Christianity's societal role.

In *The Desire of Ages*, Ellen Gould White commented on the exemplary demonstration of Jesus' worldly interactions:

Jesus had begun to break down the partition wall between Jew and Gentile, and to preach salvation to the world. Though He was a Jew, He mingled freely with the Samaritans, setting at nought the Pharisaic customs of His nation. In face of their prejudices He accepted the hospitality of this despised people. He slept under their roofs, ate with them at their tables—partaking of the food prepared and served by their hands—taught in their streets, and treated them with the utmost kindness and courtesy.

Christianity's fundamental societal role is to provide an alternative value system for heart transformation. This is the intent and nature of the Gospel. There is no other agenda. It is surely not to be illusive and or undetectable in the world. The alternative value system presented by Christianity is distinctively virtuous, relevant, effectively different, uncompromisingly empathetic, and sympathetically confrontational to existing non-Christian values. That agenda is motivated by the soul of Christianity, love to God, and love to humankind.

Two distinguished transgenerational symbols have established the indisputable function of Christianity in the world. Christianity is categorically identified as the salt and light of the earth. However, there are two challenges threatening the effectiveness of their function: salt losing its savor and light being hidden. Can salt really get contaminated? Is it even remotely possible to do so? How can light be hidden? Let me take you further.

Salt in Scripture

According to *Encyclopedia Britannica,* salt (NaCl) or sodium chloride is a mineral substance that is significantly essential to human and animal health as well as to manufacturing. Table salt, for example, is used universally as a seasoning agent. Iodized salt—that is, salt to which small quantities of potassium iodide have been added—is widely used in areas where iodine is lacking from the diet, a deficiency that can cause swelling of the thyroid gland, which is commonly called goiter. Livestock also requires salt; it is often made available in solid blocks.

In the chemical industry, salt is required in the manufacture of sodium bicarbonate (baking soda), sodium hydroxide (caustic soda), hydrochloric acid, chlorine, and many other chemicals. Salt is also employed in soap, glaze, and porcelain enamel manufacture and enters into metallurgical processes as a flux (a substance promoting fusing of metals). Salt, when applied to snow or ice, lowers the melting point of the mixture. Thus, large amounts are used in northern climates to help reduce snow and ice accumulation on roads. Salt is used in water-softening equipment that removes calcium and magnesium compounds from water.

Salt has transformative power. It is one of the four essential ingredients in bread. The valuable dough constitutes flour, salt, yeast, and water. The functions of salt in baking include stabilizing the yeast fermentation rate, strengthening the dough, enhancing the flavor of the final product, and increasing dough mixing time. Salt is also known to increase sweetness and mask metallic, bitter, or other unattractive flavors, the absence of which presents a tasteless baked product.

As the salt penetrates the dough and releases its authentic value, derived only from its source, even so must Christianity impact society. It is by effecting change that the authenticity of the Christian believer is known and not simply by the name he or she bears. Hence the need to reprimand salt over the loss of its savor (soul). Jesus spoke of the functionality of salt in the context of transformation and its ineffectiveness if it does not maintain its authenticity. He understood that the ineffectiveness of salt is just as possible as effectiveness in its lifetime. Herein lies the unconventional paradigm of Jesus:

> But if the salt have lost his savor, wherewith shall it be salted? It is thenceforth good for nothing, but to be cast out, and to be trodden under foot of men. (Matthew 5:13 ASV)

The effectiveness of the salt is in its ability to effect change, to enhance flavor, and to strengthen whichever form of preparation. The salt is effective when it has penetrated the dough.

Light in Scripture

Again, light is used as a penetrative and transformative instrument symbolic of Christianity in society.

> Ye are the light of the world. A city that is set on a hill cannot be hid. Neither do men light a candle, and put it under a bushel, but on a candlestick; and it giveth light unto all that are in the house. Let your light so shine before men, that they may see your good works, and glorify your Father which is in heaven. (Matthew 5:14–16 (KJV)

The concern shared in the scriptures includes the desire to obscure the illumination of light. "You," referring to the special team of disciples and adherents of Jesus' teachings, "are the light of the world" (Matthew 5:16).

The disciples and followers then, as is expected now, are to be agents of change. The authenticity of the agenda is indisputable. The effectiveness of the agenda, however, is not in the professing but in the effecting of Christianity's mission. It is in fulfilling the mandate of transformation that a Christian can truly say, "I have satisfied my calling."

Light has presence. The light has no business being under a bushel, as Christianity has no business retreating to inactivity, quietness, and self-preservation in a self-serving, confusing, demoralizing, impersonal, selfish, and chaotic world. The light is most effective when and where it can be seen. Any action outside of providing much-needed light to the dark surrounding is off script for Christianity and registers irrelevance to any assumed agenda. The light needs to be removed from under the bushel. The light needs to penetrate the darkness, giving true evidence of its nature. The lives of many nonbelieving would have been different if the core value of Christianity were allowed to penetrate the world around us.

Light establishes safety for socialization. We feel better when our children play in places where there is much light. We prefer to have much light around us when night falls. Conversely, unless there is an ulterior or sinister motive, socialization is always preferred in light. I can support that principle with the scriptures.

> And this is the condemnation, that light is come into the world, and men loved darkness rather than light, because their deeds were evil. (John 3:19 KJV)

The Fear of Spiritual Contamination

If salt and light have been established as functional representations of Christianity, why is there a fear of spiritual contamination? Let's venture out to 1 John 2:15–17 (KJV):

> Love not the world, neither the things that are in the
> world. If any man love the world, the love of the Father

is not in him. For all that is in the world, the lust of the flesh, and the lust of the eyes, and the pride of life, is not of the Father, but is of the world. And the world passeth away, and the lust thereof: but he that doeth the will of God abideth for ever.

Christianity teaches the essential need to separate from a world contracted with evil for a world with renewed spirituality, void of selfishness and destructive values. The belief that interaction with the world is spiritually contaminating is a pervasive reality among most Christian denominations. So pervasive is the belief that 1 John 2:15–17 (AKJV) is used to promote exclusivism in all areas of life, including in worship.

Contamination, it is believed by some, will be a reality if Christians socialize with non-Christians. Although not always immediate, the initiation, it is concluded, must be avoided at all costs. On the other hand, some Christians believe that association with non-Christians must only take place for proselytization and that, still cautiously. This position has fueled segregated schools, villages, churches, and cult-oriented colonies. I am in no way here expressing that Christianity should be deemed a cult religion. There is in every religion, Christianity included, a philosophical level of fanaticism that can fuel irrational passion and destructive patterns, utilizing theological dogmas to establish exclusivism. I am contending that Christians should intentionally interact with their world if the message of salvation is to be authentically relevant.

Fear of contamination is a disservice to the urgency of satisfying Jesus' love to the unsaved. All man-made restraints should be lifted for the advancement of the Gospel of peace. Christ's example should be followed, placing behind us the fear of being contaminated. The converted heart will drive the actions of the saved.

Ellen White's Southern Worker relates the principles and manners of Jesus and provides great support for the elimination of fear in the hearts of Christians, especially in the work of winning souls, which remains the heartbeat of the Christian faith:

Jesus while in this world ate with publicans and sinners, and mingled with the common people, not to become

47

low and earthly with them, but in order by precept and example to present to them right principles, to lift them up from their low habits and manners. In all this He set us an example, that we should follow in His steps.

Christians should demonstrate their love for humanity even when conversion to particular beliefs is not the interest of those being assisted. Christians are to get actively involved in the development of their society and intentionally give salt for the transformation of the city where they live:

> But seek the welfare of the city where I have sent you into exile, and pray to the Lord on its behalf, for in its welfare you will find your welfare. (Jeremiah 29:7 NRSV)

It is evident that the prophets demanded the active participation of religious leaders, including prophets, in the public deconstruction of moral decadence as the test of true and practical religion. The inner thoughts of the prophets were heard in the discourses of systemic reconstruction for the moral and social soul of the society. There was no private piety partitioned for temple or civic duties. Active participation in the development of the society was evident in public and private life. This exemplary model is lacking from the walls of Christian churches today.

Christians are to be living advocates for the preservation of the souls of humankind, regardless of race, color, lifestyle, or creed. The heart of humankind can only be won through the divine principle of love: love for God and love for humanity.

So, the dilemma is not in the text but in its application. The application has been structured to meet the preferences of religious socializations and doctrinal positions. A personal preference for or against a particular social interaction should not substitute the magnanimous power of love. Never should the heart be occupied with personal preferences that are made to override the agenda of Christianity.

Luke 4:17–18 (NLT) is the quintessential application of Christianity:

> The Spirit of the Lord is upon me, for he has anointed me to bring Good News to the poor. He has sent me to

proclaim that captives will be released, that the blind will
see, that the oppressed will be set free, and that the time
of the Lord's favor has come.

Like light and salt, the Christian must penetrate the world. Christianity's
agenda is to promote the liberation of humankind from slavery of all sorts,
from captivities of all times, from failures of all depth, and from allegiances
of all kinds. This means that the believer is not self-motivated to produce
another agenda or alter the mandate already established by Jesus Christ
after whom Christianity is patterned. The believer does not emphasize
individualistic Christianity but national morality. Shake some salt. When
the inspiration and agenda of the kingdom of God are better understood
by Christians, then the self-preservation veil will be lifted from the Gospel
of Jesus and the ethos of the holistic Gospel will be felt. Those principles,
at the core of Christianity, will stir discomfort in the hearts of its followers
who are knowledgeable of racial injustices, predatory business practices,
unfair wages, parasitic labor laws, and living with indifference in the cities
where they reside.

The Christian church must surrender to its mission and get rid of
its fear of contamination. Embedded in the mission of the church is the
urgency of humanity's salvation. If the church, therefore, does not become
proactive in salvaging the welfare of the city, it will lose its relevance to its
society, and its message, though revered and inspired, will lose its impact.

The deterioration and disintegration of society, with modernity a
facade, will always remain a moral and spiritual challenge for the Christian
church. As the trend continues, the church, of necessity, must challenge
itself to rise above the threshold of liturgy to the restoration and liberation
of systemically broken people in need of fresh revelations from God.

If the church is to rise to that challenging need, its inner struggles—of
accommodation for systemic injustices—must be overcome, and a sober
reflection of the voice of Jesus must be heard from the mouths of those
who claim to be salt for the salting of the earth:

But if the salt has lost its savor, it is henceforth good for
nothing, but to be cast out and to be trodden under the
feet of men. (Matthew 5:16 AKJV)

The voice of the prophet will be heard casting judgment at the church when it fails to be actively salting the earth (Jeremiah 29:7 AKJV). Likewise, the rebuke of Jesus for the barren fig tree (Matthew 21:18–19 AKJV) will be a justifiable reproach to the church. Only when the church catches a fresh understanding of its prophetic calling of being salt to disintegrating communities can its moral authority become functional, its prophetic voice become relevant, and its redemptive power become a coveted experienced.

Contamination, therefore, is not because of social interaction with nonbelievers. Contamination happens when the elements of salt and light and the virtues of morality and justice lay silent, and when immorality is allowed to fester. The controversy is over the contamination of virtues and values and not social interaction. It is about making proper representation of Christlike values in every area of life.

Vindication for the Christian will only be experienced when the functions of salt and light are evident to the world. The efficacy of those elements and virtues cannot be felt if their potential remains in isolation. Even the most detestable of preparations will need some salt. Christians, where are you to help? Bring out the saltshaker!

Illustration

"Sir, I need help. I am not an Adventist. I am not even a Christian. I don't go to church, and I don't own a Bible. I don't consider myself to be of any particular religious faith. I want to change my life, but I'm afraid I will lose my interests in sporting activities as I've seen in my friends who are members of your church. Why is it you guys don't let them get involved in competitions? When I was younger, I use to like going to church with my aunt, but when I discovered your church was not for the competitions, I lost interest. I still believe in God though."

The illustration above is a type of interaction that contends between the ambiguity of personal preference and the efficacy of the Gospel. Many would like to have the support of their religious community in all areas of their lives, but it will not always be given. Christians, however, should have an appreciation for biblically supported diversity. The Christian should recognize the significance of gifts and skill sets in the development of the community and encourage it. This includes the sporting world.

Christian values, when exposed, will transform the hearts of nonbelieving associates and they too will become saltshakers and light bearers for the Gospel. It is about being ambassadors for the inestimable values of Christ and not a contaminant for the adversary. It is the recognition of virtues that should not be hidden from society:

> [We are God's ambassadors] because we understand our fearful responsibility to the Lord, we work hard to persuade others. God knows we are sincere, and I hope you know this, too. (2 Corinthians 5:11 NLT)

> So we are Christ's ambassadors; God is making his appeal through us. We speak for Christ when we plead, "Come back to God!" (2 Corinthians 5:20 NLT)

Fear of contamination can be learned from the pulpit—about who God is and what God expects from his disciples. Many Protestant churches preach "a hell (Gehenna) to shun and a heaven to gain" message. I cannot speak to your reaction when or if you have heard those types of messages preached from the sacred desk. However, I can tell you—as a Protestant myself—that the consistency of that rhetoric without the practice of "being salt" or "being light" only distances the believer from his or her post of duty.

If I were an advocate for exclusivism, I would cheer the segregationist approach to the preaching of the Gospel. It would widen the chasm between the believing and the unbelieving and make more difficult, opportunities for authentic witnessing. However, since I am not, my support is for the body of Christ to recognize that it does not need to add authentication to the Gospel. It has been authenticated. It bears the authenticity of the One who gave it and must be allowed to be its *best* witness. I am further emphasizing that the doctrines of every Christian church, as should be rightly extracted from the Bible, the only rule of faith for the Christian, should be virtues that demonstrate one's commitment to God's truth and not the preferences of congregants or those waiting to be attracted. Such a commitment will bear fruit in all areas of the Christian's life.

Fear of spiritual contamination obscures the agenda of the Gospel of

Jesus Christ. Doctrines and traditions are in many churches, emphasized over the applied theme of the scripture: love for God and love for humankind. Further, doctrines are often used for bashing congregants over what is reasoned to be a lack of desirability for spiritual growth in their lives. (Walk with me here). Much emphasis has been placed on doing what the agent should be doing and not on being the one to do what the agent should be doing. There is an emphasis on behavior modification and not heart transformation— even when the latter is the motivation used to promote a change of lifestyle. The praxis of the Gospel is often sidelined by the emphasis of doctrines; a culture of fear is created, and members are socialized to use the paradigm of fear for God and not reverence for Him.

Fear of appearing unconverted inhibits some spiritual leaders to admit that those who love God— and who desire public demonstration of their love for Him—struggle with virtues, vices, customs, desires, orientations, or preferences as evident in humanity. Fear of getting labeled motivates others to disassociate with sinners who congregants impetuously oppose and won't allow in their church.

> # Develop the discipline to grow in grace. Grace is only given to imperfects. Perfects have no need for grace.

For example, Kelly was interested in being a member of a church that emphasized the teachings of Jesus, that demonstrated a passion for justice, that drew no racial boundaries, and that embraced all ethnicities. He was a professional and loved interacting with his membership. There was just one hurdle to get over. Kelly was a closet homosexual. Before getting exposed to religious doctrines, Kelly felt comfortable interacting with others at charitable functions and gatherings where the love of Jesus seemed to have been practically shared. Despite his lifestyle, he regularly attended services, took part in the liturgy, and served meals to the poor and homeless. Kelly was a member of a Protestant church that was homophobic. Kelly felt wounded when he heard Christians using venomous words to describe homosexuals and their preference to have homosexuals stay away from their church.

Here are some of the issues that Kelly and many others face.

Churches preach acceptance of Jesus Christ, the Son of God as the "get out of jail free" card, but they are unwilling to facilitate the work of the Gospel in the lives of those who Jesus came to save. As a matter of fact, many churches inadvertently select the orientation and assign status to their membership through their teachings, promotions, and locations.

The Gospel is to be preached to sinners, but it is not always made available to them by those who claim to be commissioned to teach it. For as long as there is a world, there will be sinners. You and I are inherently sinful. So, as long as there are sinners, the church has to embrace the idea of including in its saved membership, struggling sinners, and not set a de facto quota for the sinners who will be accepted or rejected from society. I am a firm believer that Jesus despises injustice and sins of all kind, but He completely loves the sinner. Any evidence to the contrary is a falsification of the liberating Gospel of Jesus Christ.

Exclusivism negatively impacts open access to the heart of the Gospel: Jesus Christ. The Gospel teaches an immediate surrender to God through Jesus Christ. He promises a total acceptance of the sinner who comes to Him; in Him, the sinner will find the resources for total life transformation. Why, then, should some be welcomed into the doors of the church and others be socially rejected because of the fear that they are spiritually unfit for church fellowship?

Fear of contamination has kept many churches from opening

their doors to faithfully struggling sinners. Contamination is often compartmentalized. Sexual sins have maintained the first place for most grievous sin in most, if not all, Christian churches. This includes the practice of homosexuality. The church, for the most part, is homophobic in its orientation, cautionary in its application of grace, and impractical in the spiritual expectations of its membership. Doctrinal apostasy is second, financial impropriety is third, and worship infractions are fourth.

Christians tend to forget that they, like "the would-be converted," have been commanded to grow in grace and in the knowledge of our Lord and Savior Jesus Christ (2 Peter 3:18 KJV). Growing requires patience, time, effort, determination, resilience, and proper soil conditions. The church has a pivotal role to play in the entire growth process of the one who comes to God through the power of the Holy Spirit. The growth will take place as the converting sinner spends more time with Jesus in prayer and Bible study, acquiring knowledge and developing faith. Members will make mistakes. Members may intentionally alter their decisions to walk with God. Every member should not be expected to grow at the same pace. Much more time may have to be spent with some than others. Others may require more resources and commitment on the part of the church, as well, in order to experience that desired growth. The member struggling with drug addiction or other addictive vices comes to mind.

Many churches emphasize salvation as an individual matter, but they fail to allow interests to take responsibility for their salvation. Personal responsibility must be taken for getting contaminated or experiencing spiritual growth. No one can make changes for another. You have to want to grow. You have to want to stay pure. You must possess the resolve that you will find the necessary resources to sustain your spiritual growth. The first step is to accept that there will be times when your spiritual energy will be lower than the much-needed capacity for growth. You will not always be motivated to want to grow every day. You, however, must develop the discipline to keep growing. There is no other way. You grow—or you die.

Many pretend to have forgotten that they were once nonbelievers. They really fear spiritual contamination. To those, I prayerfully encourage you to not fear that you are *imperfect* and susceptible to spiritual contamination. I hope you will not contend too long with me on that statement and realize how vulnerable you are to yourself. So, again I say, do not fear that you are *not* perfect (to be discussed much later in this book). The insatiable quest for perfection has led to the demise of many would-have-been hall of faith famers. The faster you accept that statement, the more immediate will be your psychological, social, financial, and spiritual benefits. Develop the discipline to grow in grace. Grace is only given to imperfects. Perfects don't need grace.

Christians, spiritual sojourners, and believers need to develop patience. Learn to be patient with yourself despite the possibility of spiritual contamination. You just need to develop the raw materials that you have. Stop fearing that you are not where you ought to have been. Admittedly, you may not be where you anticipated, but you have a responsibility to yourself first to grow or die spiritually. Demonstrably, take time to patiently nurture yourself. Nurture what you want to enjoy in nature. The mere desiring of growth, expansion, productivity, and admiration will not make any of the desirables a reality in your life. Those products are paid for with hard currency, such as spiritual devotion, prayer, fasting, and spiritual disciplines. Those currencies demand disciplined and laborious effort on your part.

The church community must develop and demonstrate patience as must individual members. Growth does require appreciable patience on the part of both the church and member. Failure on the part of either party will negatively impact what should be a dynamic growth process:

> For a just man falleth seven times, and riseth up again: but the wicked shall fall into mischief. (Proverbs 24:16 AKJV)

> For though the righteous fall seven times, they rise again, but the wicked stumble when calamity strikes. (Proverbs 24:16 NIV)

> The godly may trip seven times, but they will get up again. But one disaster is enough to overthrow the wicked. (Proverbs 24:16 NLT)

The church should expect shortcomings and intentional lapses in the spiritual life of its membership. After all, this is one of the foundational reasons for the community of believers to nurture the spiritual life of all believers.

The "just" one, in assessing their state, may be shameful of the fall or the circumstances surrounding it. Each fall, though appearing similar, has marked differences. The second fall may be different from the first, and the fourth may be significantly harsher and more spiritually debilitating than the third. The rise from each fall may require various calibers of support. It may just be that shame and guilt have deepened their grip on an already weakened heart. Nevertheless, the sinner, in solitude, recognizes the destructiveness of each fall but remains resolute to continue getting up and dusting off the dust of the falls. The sinner does it over and over again. That priceless attitude forms the basis of the movement from practicing to saved sinner.

The saved sinner, though experienced in falling, is greater in overcoming. The saved sinner confesses, repents, and overcomes. The practicing sinner remains in the fallen situation despite the available way out.

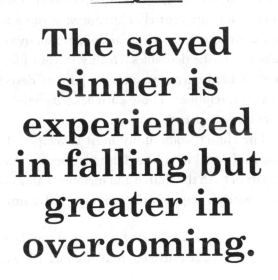

The saved sinner is experienced in falling but greater in overcoming.

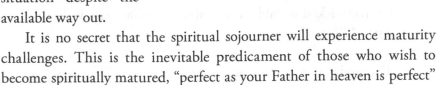

It is no secret that the spiritual sojourner will experience maturity challenges. This is the inevitable predicament of those who wish to become spiritually matured, "perfect as your Father in heaven is perfect" (Matthew 5:48 AKJV). The much-quieted truth is the acceptance of the maturity challenges. The established reality is that those who are seriously committed to their spiritual journey and determined to venturing onward will be buffeted with distracting experiences along the way. There is no limit to their potential and actual setbacks. Doubts will motivate curiosity, temptations will precede transgressions, and disappointment and pain may succeed the well-intentioned or ill-intentioned diversion. Hence the absolute need to remain committed to the relationship.

The sinner's attitude toward victorious living marks the significant difference between their salvation or condemnation. Both individuals are born sinners as accepted by David (Psalm 51:5 AKJV). Both individuals fall to their proclivities fueled by their propensity and desires to sin. Both have fallen short of the grace of God (Romans 3:23 AKJV). The stark difference, however, between the saved sinner and the practicing sinner is the refusal to sustain a spiritually destructive behavior.

It is important to establish that attitude is the sole determinant to establish or cancel all victories in your life. Instead of remaining focused on having fallen, the potential victor engages all energies into continuing the intended journey. This is instrumental in setting a foundation and transforming character. The destiny of the potential overcomer remains an illusion until the attitude toward failure changes. Oftentimes, it is the preoccupation with spectators that defeats the rise to the altitude of phenomenal achievements. Make the effort to cancel that defeatist attitude and experience the changes that will leap you from the valley of despondency to the mountain of hope and the rock of spiritual maturity.

Falling is not much the spiritual conflict as not rising. The conflict is in the falling and rising. The failure is in not rising. It's immaterial how many times you fall if you keep rising each time you do. Both the righteous and the unrighteous fall. Remain determined that whenever you fall, publicly or privately, that you will continue to grope your way forward. That is the quintessential difference:

- If I (you) fall
- I (You) rise back up.
- If I (You) fail
- I (You) try again.

What must be the attitude of the "un-fallen" or the "not-yet-fallen" toward the fall of their enemy?

> Rejoice not when thine enemy falleth, and let not thine heart be glad when he stumbleth: lest the Lord see it, and it displease him, and he turn away his wrath from him. (Proverbs 24:17–18 AKJV)

The scriptures exhort the "un-fallen" or the "not-yet-fallen" to remain sensitive to the fall of an enemy. Why? In 1 Corinthians 10:12 (AKJV), the apostle Paul gives us the profound answer:

> Wherefore let him that thinketh he standeth take heed lest he fall.

This reestablishes Jesus's protocol for healthy Christian living:

> But I say unto you, "Love your enemies, bless them that curse you, do good to them that hate you, and pray for them which despitefully use you, and persecute you; that ye may be the children of your Father which is in heaven: for he maketh his sun to rise on the evil and on the good, and sendeth rain on the just and on the unjust." (Matthew 5:44–45 AKJV)

Be the type of sojourner who, despite past failures, will keep trekking forward.

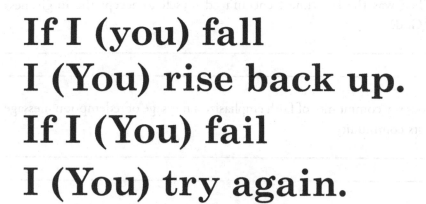

If I (you) fall
I (You) rise back up.
If I (You) fail
I (You) try again.

ASSESSMENT QUESTIONS

When was the last time I encouraged myself to accept the forgiveness of God?

_____

_____

Does my community of faith emphasize a message of redemption message to its community?

_____

_____

Am I fearful of being a Christian in my society? What reasons do I have to be fearful?

_____

_____

Am I patient with myself? How much?

_____

_____

Have I considered the cost of impatience in my personal spiritual life?

_____

_____

What about spiritual contamination that concerns or scares me?

_____

_____

Am I growing spiritually? How do I know that I am? What evidence says I am growing?

_____

_____

Life is not going to give to the weak What belongs to the strong.

—Anonymous

CHAPTER 5

Fear: The Motivator?

Fear is an active enemy combatant. My childhood experience with God was markedly different from my present walk with Him. My childhood experiences were shaped principally by fear and little faith. I feared punishment, both from my parents and God. I was afraid of God. I was afraid of God to the point that I did not want to approach anything that had to do with spirituality until I believed I had everything perfect with God. I had to have done everything right even to think of approaching Him.

I feared getting struck by God's fury as retaliation for my repeated sins and weaknesses. Quite frankly, I do not know any other origin for that belief except my family, my church, my school, and my community. I should point out I attended a Christian denominational school. My family belonged to the same church whose school I attended. I rarely interacted with non-SDAs in my community except when I would be inviting them (mind you, the same ones I hardly interacted with) to church or church-related activities.

Fear controlled my childhood. It was an enemy combatant, and it still is. If I were writing this book in my teens, I certainly would not have said, "Fear is an assigned enemy combatant commissioned to engage us in surreptitious distraction en route to the fulfillment of our assignment." I would not have made that statement, in retrospect, because I grew up in a conservative yet abusive context where fear was the sole raison d'être for doing anything. Fear of punishment drove me to the river to fetch water at the times—I believe—I should have been able to play.

Fear drove me to school because I was afraid I would not have satisfied the academic expectations of those closest to me and their confidence in me. Although I saw education as my way out of my abusive situation, I had no clue how I would accomplish that goal. Ambivalence drove me to church because it provided a recess from the toxicity of the home and an opportunity to fellowship with others. At church, I indulged myself in participation out of interest for salvation. Hellfire was definitely not the option. (Even if I had chosen to believe it was not real, my fear of its reality at the end of my life was not allayed by the manner it was presented at church). After worship services on Sabbaths, especially, I looked forward to having guests at home for lunch, even if we did not have much. We always seemed to have had enough to share; at least my mother made it seem so.

Outside of the church service context, school was the avenue for academic and psychological reprieve. Attending the Saint Lucia Seventh-day Adventist Academy was a cathartic season. Learning was not fun at all times, but it was necessary. Assignments were interpreted as grilling and not understanding their contribution to my future academic goals. I knew nothing about college or college life except that it was more school—much harder than where I was—and that it would teach me how to preach and make me a pastor.

Quite honestly, I only knew there was one college to choose from and to attend: Caribbean Union College. It was the only college I heard my church speak about. I did not know there were other colleges or universities in the world. Since both of my parents and my siblings only had elementary school education, the thought of reaching the walls of another academic institution was a phenomenal dream that only history could truly explain. I was afraid that God would allow me that opportunity only if I had done everything perfectly, and I tried to do just that. Needless to say, I failed miserably at that goal.

My social interaction outside of home and church was a disaster. When I got to school, I was always challenged with socialization because I feared rejection and the contamination of my spiritual goals by persons who were different from me. Differences in religious beliefs, mannerisms, academic intelligence, and social skills were significant to me. I guarded that type of information. Tempted to share it? Yes, I was. Willing to do so? Nope! Would never have volunteered that information. I feared becoming like the world. I feared not being "the salt of the earth" (Matthew 5:13 AKJV) or being "the light of the world," shining my light before all people (Matthew 5:14, 16 AKJV). I feared not having friends and not "showing myself friendly" (Proverbs 18:24 AKJV) because I did not have the habit of socializing with persons outside of immediate family, relatives who lived close by, or church members.

Fear of mingling with the world motivated me to avoid the development of potential meaningful friendships. I genuinely thought that friendship with persons outside of the Seventh-day Adventist Church was enmity with God. I lacked the motivation to step outside of that understanding. I was sold out on the perverted scriptural interpretations such as 1 John 2:15 (AKJV) that emphasized "love not the world, neither the things that are in the world; if any man loves the world, the love of the father is not in him," 1 John 2:15 (AKJV), and 2 Corinthians 6:14 (AKJV), not yoking with unbelievers, and avoiding fellowship with darkness. The misuse of those texts was entirely damning, segregating, and promoting religious bigotry, social phobias, and "otherworldly" attitudes to

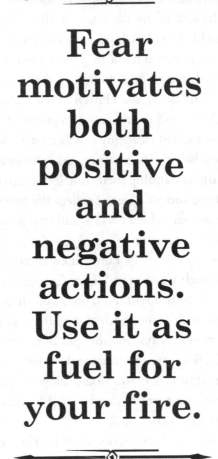

Fear motivates both positive and negative actions. Use it as fuel for your fire.

me. I became very aware of the intention of the text as I grew older. Nevertheless, the sensitization of other worldliness had impacted much of my few friendships and my walk with God.

In addition to the impact of religious bigotry, I was afraid to fail in every area of my life. I was afraid that I'd disappoint my church, my teachers, my parents, and my siblings who believed I was destined to become a pastor. Never did I realize that the seed of fear had been planted in my life and that the circumstances of my childhood watered its growth. I knew I wanted to get out of my abusive childhood situation, but I didn't know how.

When I heard chatter about the college in Trinidad that prepared young men *(no women spoken of then although females did attend)* for ministry, I was excited because I understood something was different about me even then, and that something was God's calling on my life to the Gospel ministry. Now, that excited me. It was my way of using my fear as fuel for my future success. I am still interpreting this anomaly today.

Fear can fuel a way out of potential failure. Fear, conversely, leads to failure—but only if you let it. Fear, by nature, immobilizes. However, when arrested, its passion for derailment can be redirected to motivate. Yes, it can if you understand it! Fear can fuel the desire for greatness. That's what I discovered. My recognition was that I had innate potential that needed to be used to achieve what I felt was my destiny.

> # Fear can fuel a way out of potential failure. Fear, conversely, leads to failure— but only if you let it.

This was my great motivation: if I would walk out of my abusive situation, I needed to succeed beyond the expectations of those who believed in me. I had to do it for myself—beyond what my elementary-schooled parents, teachers, church leaders, and siblings saw in me. I had to stand on the shoulders that stood in position, at my disposal, for my success.

Fear motivates actions that are both positive and negative. Fear can fuel a way out of potential failure and can lead to failure. This is an expression of experience for me and a siren signal for you. What happens from here will be determined by you. Fear's agenda is to immobilize your responses to the very things that you need to survive. It is pointless seeking to believe it has another agenda. Its nature is to constrict until it suffocates the last breath out of you.

Have you ever been afraid to take an examination because you were not sufficiently ready to take it? As the day approaches, fear grips your heart, and anxiety winds up your emotions. Fear of failing that examination drives you to your textbooks for more revision, potentially resulting in the necessary pass on results day. So, it needs to be the same in every area of your life. Get the work done if you want to shine.

Fear can motivate the fulfillment of negative prophecies in our lives. Were you ever told you would not amount to anything good, that your life would be gloomy and unattractive, that you would not be a success story, or that you would repeat your ancestors' history? Demotivating, right? Judgmental, right? Of course, it is. But the very tenet and context of the statement, with all the possible explanations and juxtapositions, should be used to fuel your motivation to hunker down, reassess your life, and set projections with a trajectory toward a successful future. Fear of fulfilling that statement needs to fuel your passion to succeed because your future depends on it. Your legacy is on the line. Your story is unfinished and needs to have a bright ending. Use the fear of acquiescing to the sentiments of your distractor to motivate your resilience for greater skill development, deeper compassion in problem-solving, and to be more embracing of diversity without demoralizing your values. Fuel your compunction to challenge weaknesses in you, both subtle and evident, and let those prognostications against your life serve as fuel for a fulfilling journey.

Fear impacts everything you allow. Fight it! Fear must always be used as a catalyst to a regenerative experience. Fear, that intense emotion aroused by the detection of an imminent threat to your future, your family, or your legacy, must be used to motivate you into action. Let the shame of an unimproved future trigger the necessary physiological changes that will springboard you into action. It should be so because your life depends on the decisions you make. A fulfilling legacy depends on it as well.

Have you ever heard a friend or family member relating your life experience to another, and the testimony you would have left behind? As I write this chapter, I am reminded of the words of a song: "Don't let me leave behind an unfinished task." Unconsciously the motivations of that song have always fueled my passion to live a life that is sufficiently beneficial to others and to myself. A daunting task it has been and will remain. It is a fulfillment of the words of Jesus: "Love your neighbor as yourself" (Mark 12:31 NIV). Be assured, however, that just as there is a sizable crowd cheering you on to the finish line, the stands are filled with spectators who have no interests in whether you succeed or fail. As you journey through that race, pay greater attention to finishing well than being a good sport for a disinterested spectator.

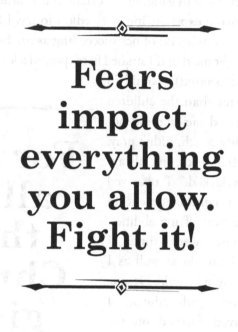

Fears impact everything you allow. Fight it!

Remember to put in the work if you want to shine. Fear can frame a negative interpretation to every experience that you allow it to. The permission for fear to reign in your life, to be or to do, is a daily decision that you need to make.

Fear fuels anxiety; pay attention! I've lived through that phase. That fearful phase. I've always been afraid to fail. I was told by my father that failure lives next door to us and that I should not befriend it. Despite all his shortcomings, for he has many, my father planted that universal seed of resilience in me. Inspired by the constant stories of his challenging childhood, I was determined to change the trajectory of my life. I was afraid of disappointing my father. I was afraid of disappointing God. There were times when I was more afraid of disappointing my father than I was of disappointing God. Strange, you may say, but my understanding of God was that He had wrath and forgiveness at the same time. I was not always successful in gauging the extent of my father's anger, and I tried very hard to avoid experiencing it. Needless to say, I failed many times.

I was afraid of not succeeding as my father told me that I should. He taught me that if I studied hard, prayed a lot, read a lot, and didn't "skylark" (fool around), I would do better than the children around me who did not study much, didn't pray, didn't read, and always "skylarked." I observed that commandment to the best of my abilities. There were times I did not do as well as I thought I would. Despite those infractions, I stayed focused on the motivation behind my father's commandment: "You need to succeed." That, for me, decades later, more than then, was a priceless gift.

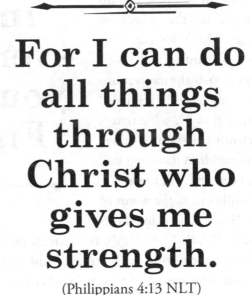

For I can do all things through Christ who gives me strength.

(Philippians 4:13 NLT)

Fear of disappointing God, at times, drove me to isolation. It was as if the thought of not pleasing God was directly linked to the reality of engaging my father's anger. Surely, I always hoped that the standard would be lowered a little, but it wasn't. The bar was kept. I look back, and I think that my baptism into the Seventh-day Adventist Christian faith had much to do with the standards set because I needed to demonstrate a spiritual walk with God.

Fear as a negative motivation will shortchange anyone's life if it is allowed. It is emphatically depressing trying to serve God and time being afraid of him at the same. It's really a frustrating experience. Additionally, it is discomfiting to the one who wants to serve God to try doing just enough to impress God and those around them at the same time. You will compromise your standards, damage yourself, ruin your identity, and develop unsavory friendships. All you have to do is to set your standard and honor it.

You need to appreciate that the gradual development of your spiritual self will reveal deeper character flaws in you. Some flaws may require greater effort to get over than others, but all will require effort on your part. You have to have confidence in God and in yourself. You have to want to win. At the same time, you have to learn to be patient with yourself.

We need to acknowledge that impatience comes from the comparison of ourselves with those around us. When we conclude that others are growing spiritually and we're not, we tend to whip ourselves with the sticks of spiritual isolation for greater penance and future restoration. The truth is that everyone will not be at the same spiritual maturity level at the same time, all of the time. Each person is different—and so is their journey with God. I encourage you to accept who you are. Work hard at not comparing yourself to others and harder at submitting who you are, what you desire, your potential, your dreams, your failures, and your successes to God. Get to experience the phenomenal truth: "With God, all things are possible" (Matthew 19:26 AKJV).

Remember to put in the work if you want to shine.

Fear makes everything seem impossible. Unfortunately, even Christians are overtaken by the presence of fear: fear of not having, fear of not being, and fear of losing. As legitimate as the emotion may be, we ought not to give the management of our lives to it. We ought never to look at problems as overwhelming. Our approach should be to handle them a little bit at a time. It's management approach will motivate us to achieve. That's God's will for you.

Here are some principles that will return incalculable dividends.

1. Stop wasting valuable time fearing omnipotence that is available to empower and transform your life. If there's something you know you have to do, get it done. Procrastination is as adversarial to success as fear is to a meaningful relationship.
2. Use all you have to do whatever your hands find to do.
3. Admit when you fear, but don't give control over to it.
4. Honor your future with single-minded boldness. How? Learn to block some things and some people out. Seriously? Emphatically yes! Everything and everyone do not belong in your future. Why? Everything and everyone will not motivate or facilitate your growth.
5. Change some of your friends. Limit your time with others, but you need to take charge of your destiny.
6. Choose your friends wisely. It's your right to do so. If you fail at that, you will fail at having success capital at your disposal and on your stage. Don't worry—choosing friends wisely is diametrically opposite to disliking another person.
7. Don't let the expectations of others contaminate you.
8. Be bold and fearless. You will not get to where God wants to take you until you decide that you will do what it requires to get there.

I was working with a company on the cutting edge of foster care. I moved from one city to the next to facilitate employment with that company. We had just had our first son. My wife was in graduate school, and we depended on my employment for our livelihood. Everything in my estimation seemed to have been going just right. I worked long hours and expended much effort to secure clientele.

When my management decisions conflicted with those at the corporate office, I was fired under the pretext of company readjustments. I was disappointed because I didn't see it coming and had planned my immediate life around my employment. I was allowed a call from my office as I was getting ready to pick up my belongings. I called my wife. When she got to the phone, I said, "The eagle has landed. It's no longer flying" Translation: "I got a blow so meaningful that I'm unable to fly." I later understood that it was a favorable move of God to get me into pastoral ministry.

Don't be mistaken. God expects us to recognize our strengths and not settle for what others think we should have or what others think we should do. Many Christians don't realize their potential because they have come to believe God expects them to be without or to have little, or to live in much adversity to decrease their accessibility to damnation. They contend Matthew 19:24 (NKJV): "And again I say unto you, it is easier for a camel to go through the eye of a needle, than for a rich man to enter into the kingdom of God."

Others misappropriate 1 Timothy 6:10 (NKJV): "For the love of money is a root of all kinds of evil, for which some have strayed from the faith in their greediness, and pierced themselves through with many sorrows." They think it means God does not want His children to achieve material wealth. So, they begin to fear wealth and the process of acquiring it. This fallacy has been long perpetuated by countless Christians as spiritual consolation for their lack of desire for wealth or frustration in not acquiring wealth that they have so long been silently asking or desiring in prayer.

Fear speaks negatively about ambition. However, there is nothing wrong with godly ambition. Don't settle for less than what God has promised you. Jeremiah 29:11 (AKJV) pronounces, "For I know the thoughts that I think toward you, saith the Lord, thoughts of peace, and not of evil, to give you an expected end."

Do not allow fear to quench your fire. Let people know that you know what you're doing and what you're about. It is the manifestation of God's blessings in your life that will highlight God in your life—and not what you say. Your fruits must show it. Matthew 7:16, 20 (AKJV) says, "Ye shall know them by their fruits. Do men gather grapes of thorns, or figs of thistles? Wherefore by their fruits ye shall know them. This principle is further supported by Matthew 5:16" (AKJV). Let your light so shine before men that they may see your good works and glorify your Father in heaven. Do not let fear distract you from such exponential growth in God.

Here I am reminded of a quotation that was read to a classmate and me, by my high school principle, who also served as my ministerial internship supervisor, after we had gotten into a classroom scuffle. It has since become one of my favourite quotes from Ellen G. White:

> Higher than the highest human thought can reach is God's ideal for His children. Godliness—godlikeness—is the goal to be reached. Before the student there is opened a path of continual progress. He has an object to achieve, a standard to attain, that includes everything good, and pure, and noble. He will advance as fast and as far as possible in every branch of true knowledge. But his efforts will be directed to objects as much higher than mere selfish and temporal interests as the heavens are higher than the earth.

Let's not forget that godly ambition motivated the preaching of the Gospel in different parts of the world (Romans 15:20 AKJV, 1 Thessalonians 4:11 AKJV). History is replete with stories of Christians traveling to different parts of the Roman Empire to share the teachings of Jesus Christ. Christians traveled as missionaries, evangelists, and builders to ensure the message of salvation was practically heard and received. Potential and commitment made it all happen—not fear!

Christians should put as much energy into the evangelization of the world as into the development of assets and dreams. Here's

Inch by inch, life's a cinch. Yard by yard, life is hard.

—Author unknown

the perennial challenge. The extremes exist in Christendom. Some argue and promote absence of ambition for wealth, and others promote obsession in acquisition of wealth, ignoring the need to honor God with all their substance. A meaningful understanding of God will not embrace either extreme; it will favor the ambitious development of our talents, gifts and skills for the advancement of our lives and the practical liberating Gospel of Jesus Christ. This is the primary imperative of Christianity.

Get that potential materialized. Your legacy awaits!

Though tainted with fear, my walk with God has been a sweet challenge. It has not been without hurdles. There have been life-threatening, financially debilitating, employment-challenging, friendship-shortlisting, sexist-equating, and emotionally rejecting hurdles. Along the way, I learned to develop an appreciation for the written Word of God and the proven friendships of humans. I've faced defeat again and again, but I made a commitment to my destiny that I intend to keep.

Although I have been whooped many times, not once have I ever decided to stop being passionate about my life and my contribution to this world. I have learned to challenge fear and believe in God. I live my legacy every day. My critic said, "You're not good enough." Others said, "You don't deserve it." Many more contended, "It's not your time." The obstacles kept coming along my way, but I have been relentless about what I believe God has ordained for me.

Fear of disappointing God motivated me to seek God. Oxymoron? I can understand if that's your interpretation. I've been there. Fear of God sent me asking God for a word that transcends culture, time, people, and traditions. I was led to Proverbs 24:16–18 (NLT):

> The godly may trip seven times, but they will get up again. But one disaster is enough to overthrow the wicked. Don't rejoice when your enemies fall; don't be happy when they stumble. For the Lord will be displeased with you and will turn his anger away from them.

Many times in the past, I have recommended those scripture verses to others, to help elevate them out of their troubles. I led them to believe, as I now do, that there is no need to surrender your destination when difficulties arise along your journey. There is no need to throw in the towel and breathe your last breath. You may have to shield the heat of the penetrating midday sun, you may have to fight gnats at dusk, and you may have to get up again and again and again because of falls taken along the way. Dust yourself off and keep trekking. Be unbroken despite the falls. Develop resilience but don't reject yourself. Your destiny awaits you. Focus on your goals. Relentlessly face each goal with dogged determination. Every fall gives you a memory that you should be motivated not to repeat. It takes courage to act and to start over and over and over again. It is not the ungodly who fall seven times. It is the righteous who fall seven times. How many times have you fallen?

Do not fear! You will have to stay focused if you want to enlarge your perception of yourself. You will have to develop your gifts and make that conscious decision to better yourself, to sharpen your skills, to readily step over your hurdles, to work hard, and to stick to your task of developing your legacy. Let nothing stop you. Talk less and work harder. Parrots are noisy, but eagles fly higher. Don't talk *big* and act small. Stop stacking up dreams and waiting for the magical season to execute them. Begin the execution today. Stockpiled dreams have no significance; they only serve as references for undeveloped potential. Let your actions do all the talking and your enemies do the "score-boarding." If this is not what you will do, then you have no reason to be doing all that talking. Persevere. In God's strength, you will attain the promise.

Be aware that your world will suddenly become different when, with tenacity, you become fearless and free your soul and others' souls from the viciousness of fear.

ASSESSMENT QUESTIONS

What plans do I have for my life?

_____

_____

Have I been working on those plans? If yes, how?

_____

_____

What other efforts must I take in other to achieve those goals?

_____

_____

What are my distractions? List them.

_____

_____

To my recollection, in what ways have I contributed to my distractions?

_____

_____

Am I in service to God and to humanity in my plans? How so?

_____

_____

Write out your commitment to keep God in your plans.

_____

_____

Remember to use fear as fuel for your passion.

CHAPTER 6

The Fear of Failure

Failure has no preference for race, status, creed, or religion. Failure is not spiritual or secular. Failure has no season, and it has no proclivity to bold or shy personalities. Promise does not secure it, and flattery does not redeem it. It knows no depth, height, or circumstance that can break its relationship with fear. Failure has no regard for those who wallow in pity and wishful thinking or drink from the cisterns of vain idealism in the valley of despair, lavishing their productive moments spectating instead of building for tomorrow today. No wonder many fear failures.

Those who walk with God are not immune to the possibility or experience of failure. You and I will fail sometimes even if we have never failed before. We may fail at what we think we're good at doing or being good at. Failure may come to us when we have our best game planned, studied long hours, or followed the letter to the T. No one is in any way inoculated from failure even after seven opportunities to improve on anything. The first opportunity to guard against failure is at the time of deciding that "I will do it."

Temporary setbacks are often the cause of despair for many would-be high achievers. They give up at the first sight or experience of setbacks. So that we understand each other and that your expectations are not disappointed, let me inform you that you should expect failure along your journey to phenomenal success. Expect that some days will not be as bright as other days. Expect that some mornings, you will not want to study for the upcoming examination. Expect that some days, you will look for your closest friends, and they will not be immediately present. On some days, the clouds will seem more permanent in your life than the sun you so readily desire. On some days, the rain will be a prolonged feature in your life. On some days, you may look at your spouse and feel disappointed about your relationship. On some days, you will not want to show up for work. On some days, you will not want to hold the hand of your spouse as you walk through romantically charged places. On some days, you will look for success, but all you will find is failure. On some days, you will be tempted to turn back from continuing your journey. The destination may seem too far away.

I remember driving back from Florida with my wife and mother-in-law after a visit to her stepdaughter. We decided to drive almost

Failure is not the presence of, but the mismanagement of, fear and temptation.

nine hundred miles without understanding how tiring it would be, especially since it was our first drive to Florida. Despite the tiredness, we needed to make it back home to Alabama. Every stop for fuel was an energizing boost. All I had on my mind was getting home. As tiring as it was, our destination remained our motivation.

As it is in the natural even more so in the spiritual. Our life's journey is similar. We need to get refueled along the way. At those times, we need not get emotionally distressed and give up. If you do, you are saying that you would not be pleased if you but survive tomorrow. In the scriptures, Jesus said that He sends the rain on both the just and the unjust. So, just because it's raining doesn't mean it's over for your plans. It doesn't mean you have suddenly become unjust or just.

Your soul has a character that speaks of who you are. It speaks loudly in difficult times. A mature character helps you manage the uncertainty of the moment. Understand that you don't have control over failure staring at you in the morning, at noon, or in the evening, but you can decide to dismiss its clamor for your embrace or you can befriend it. That's a choice you can make. That type of resilience is not developed by a mere willful ordering of mental energies. It is accomplished by faith in God.

> For in him we live and move and are! As one of your own poets says it, "We are the sons of God." (Acts 17:28 TLB)

> For in him we live and move about and exist, as even some of your own poets have said, "For we too are his offspring." (Acts 17:28 NET)

Fear gives rise to false definitions. One of those misleading definitions is failure. Failure must be differentiated from the lack of obtaining a particular goal. Although a person may not succeed at the first attempt of a goal, it is not permanent until they decide to give up on trying. To embrace discouragement and give up on trying is the quintessential definition of failure. Thankfully, the principle of failure does not only lie in what you can hear, smell, taste, see, or feel. It is in what is manageable. Visual individuals can picture and dismantle objects with their physical and philosophical eyes. Tactile individuals can also physically feel and emotionally connect to the object of care, concern, or hate. Everyone, at some time, will have the urge to pursue the object of their desire. It is the inability to achieve that particular prize that is deemed as failure, especially if a colossal cost was attached to the pursuance of that goal.

The journey to total self-awareness, self-consciousness, and self-acceptance demands the acceptance of fear as an attraction for failure. In other words, fear initiates failure. No one is immune to the features of failure—not even Christians who confess the presence of God in their lives. Christians experience relationship breakups, academic inconsistencies, financial woes, and career mishaps on a daily basis. As a matter of fact, it is not unusual that Christians have to deal with such experiences because of their religious faith. So, for the Christian, failure is not an unmentioned reality; it is an interpretation of values, processes, and expectations. Failure, for the Christian, is not the lack of achievement or the seasonal presence of fear; it is the residence of negativities in one's life. Those negativities can annihilate hope.

The fear of failure motivates many to believe that religiosity, piety, and spirituality are escapes from failure. The presence of God in the life of the Christian is often interpreted as immunity from all negative experiences that non-Christians face. In a very real way, many choose religion or a certain path to piety for absolution from potential punishment from their offensive transactions. Others seek to secure a safe seat on the lifeboat called Christianity because it is believed that Christians or believers in God will receive immunity from the degeneration around them. Those become very disenchanted with their faith when life affords them opportunities that reflect qualitative hardships.

It is impossible to provide ourselves blanket immunity from the negatives of de-generation.

This reminds me of the story of a statesman who was baptized as a Christian. Not too long after his conversion experience, he was elected as an ambassador for his country. His faith in God was reinforced until he was charged with gun trafficking. Although he was later exonerated, his faith in God was shattered for God's apparent failure to protect him from such disrepute. Not long after his exoneration, as he was walking with a friend, he broke down in tears and demanded an answer from God for such a blow to his career and reputation. It was his belief that being a Christian would have shielded him from such vicious attacks.

Spiritual sojourners also experience confusion. Many are disappointed when faced with seemingly insurmountable challenges. It is customary for others to quote Exodus 15:26 (AKJV):

> If thou wilt diligently hearken to the voice of the Lord thy God, and wilt do that which is right in his sight, and wilt give ear to his commandments, and keep all his statutes, I will put none of these diseases upon thee, which I have brought upon the Egyptians: for I am the Lord that healeth thee.

> And the Lord will take away from you all sickness, and will afflict you with none of the terrible diseases of Egypt which you have known, but will lay them on all those who hate you. (Deuteronomy 7:15 AKJV)

The implication here is that sickness is considered a mark of spiritual failure and dishonor for those who believe that Christians are beyond the reach of sickness, and that the indwelling presence of God in them provides immunity from the ailments of the world. The principle extracted here by most is that failure is not possible in the life of the believer unless there is disharmony with God. Failure is seen as punishment from God. Let me hasten to say that such dogmatism has led to a misunderstanding of God as a tyrannical despot who vindictively imposes punishment on those he disapproves, or blessings on those He favors.

Some years ago, I was confronted by a Christian after one of my radio shows. I had just completed discussion on mitigation strategies for the high suicide rate on the island of St. Lucia.

He asked, "Why are you giving the people all those exercises and things to do to deal with suicidal ideations?"

I tried explaining that some persons do not read the Bible as he does, and they need to know that we (Christians) care.

He (Christian) quickly responded, "Send all of them who feel depress and anxious to the Bible. All the answers are there so they won't want to kill themselves."

As I tried to explain, "Christians feel depress and suicidal, and it's not because they don't love God," He got angry and stormed off, leaving me standing where he had aggressively stopped me.

I'm not trying to tear down faith here. By no means! I am making the point that we have no blanket life-preserving immunity from the impact of degeneration all around us. I'm saying it is impossible to provide ourselves blanket immunity from the negatives of degeneration. Our world is consistently degenerating—and so is our physicality. What we have available to us as Christians is the guaranteed promise of God to take us through the dark valleys of unwanted sicknesses, despair, imperfections, and physical death. We have the responsibility of being true to godly virtues, opportunities, and potential in the fulfillment of God's creation intent for us.

In Genesis, we have evidence of the provisions made for all humanity. Total dominion was given to those who came from the hands of the Creator, but everything to this moment continues to deteriorate as a direct result of disobedience. Joseph was assigned a journey that was beyond the limited comprehension of his siblings. His path took him through the crucible of a dry pit, the corporate management of

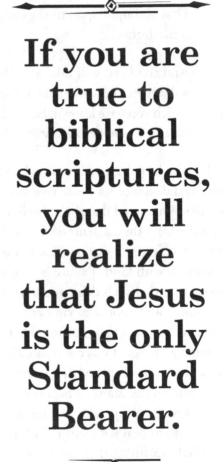

If you are true to biblical scriptures, you will realize that Jesus is the only Standard Bearer.

Potiphar's affairs, the cold walls of an Egyptian prison, and the governorship of Egypt. Job was another example of Yahweh's arbitrary decision to assign the test of faithfulness to God over family and material possessions. Daniel is worthy of mention because of his commitment to spiritual virtues and personal fulfillment over political allegiance, social correctness, and death.

To many, the trials of Joseph, Job, Daniel, and other faithful people only matter because they journeyed to a triumphant end. You and I would not have been so intrigued about them if their life accounts did not fascinate us. Imagine having no personal knowledge of them and still being interested in their failures and successes. We are fascinated by success stories, and we love to identify with successful stories. We distance ourselves from everything that appears to be failing. It's almost like penance made for personal deficiencies in related areas of our lives.

Christians should exercise spiritual caution in passing judgment on those who do not satisfy the standards they have erected. No one has the right to mete out judgment to another on the basis that someone else's walk with God does not measure up to their standards. If you are true to biblical scriptures, you will realize that Jesus is the only Standard Bearer. He is the elevator that takes us to the next level in our walk with Him. He is the moral agent who actively transforms our surrendered character to the epitome of godliness, which we desire. Herein lies the reason we should reject every tendency to portray ourselves as the ultimate example for anyone to emulate.

As mannered, disciplined, schooled, economically sufficient, and relationship exemplary as you may be, guard against elevating yourself as the standard bearer. Why? Even the best of rose plants carry thorns in their bodies. If you are true to biblical scripture, you will realize that the God-Man Jesus is the only Standard Bearer.

I encourage everyone to seek the wisdom of God in an effort to understand the dilemmas of those who suffer with illnesses, financial hardships, dysfunctional relationships, emotional instabilities, and spiritual warfare. They are either victims of their own decisions or the decisions of others. Personal decisions, even selfish ones, may result in extenuating consequences. It should not be the early conclusion of fallible beings who have no control or power over the next moment of their lives that God has forgotten about the distressed, oppressed, or downtrodden. Yahweh can assign, designate, castigate, and elevate those He has chosen to be His vessels. He does it in His time, for His glory, and for the fortifying of our faith in Him.

With that being said, let me ask the burning question. How does one fail as a Christian? Is it even remotely possible for a Christian to fail? Is a Christian allowed to fail? What is failure for the Christian? These are three of the most significant questions that can be asked about the faithfulness of a believer in Jesus Christ. Bearing in mind that a Christian is a believer in the birth, life, death, burial, resurrection, and restoration of all things in Jesus, the issue of commitment to that ideology is crucial in the perpetuation of those beliefs. It is also instrumental in the conversion of contrary thinkers to the Christian faith community.

Failure for the Christian is not the presence of temptation or fear. These are invariable elements of distraction on the Christian's journey. Failure is the misappropriation of faith to overcome the elements that contravene Christian values and militate the desire to walk with God. Though frequently bombarded with temptations and fears to the contrary of their faith, the Christian is not forgotten by God or banished from the throne room of God, where grace and mercy is actively dispensed to all who ask.

Failure is not missing the mark but the decision to refuse help to attain to the mark of the high calling in Jesus Christ. Failure is the inability to manage the process sufficiently well, losing sight of the goal, which is to produce the expected outcome. The most significant of all expected outcomes for every believer is immortality: eternal life in Jesus. Therefore, there is a need to challenge the determination of fear to fight the process.

The Christian's advantage is to acknowledge that fear itself is limited. It is only as powerful as the one who embraces it. Therefore, to overcome any distraction summoned by fear, you need to apply the weapon of faith. Know, however, that faith is not a drug that expunges commitment and determination. The value of beliefs fosters diligence, allegiance, and fidelity to the process of spiritual success.

Faith recognizes the possibility of failure. Recognition is not failure. It is the opposite. It is a victory. Accepting who you are is more beneficial to you and others than believing you are who you are not. Own yourself. Remember that! Faith does not deny weaknesses that can lead to failure.

Rather, it embraces present deficiencies and works for that which will please God. The deciding factor is our diligence to continue walking with God despite the cost. Faith says, "I have an allegiance to the values that motivate the stronger bond to spiritual relationship building." Faith says, "I am committed to the promise even when the situation appears despairingly impossible." Faith says, "My weaknesses are obvious, yet my victory is assured if I but stand up to my weaknesses and deny them their pleasures."

In *Faith and Works,* Ellen Gould White penned the process in these words:

> The sinner may err, but he is not cast off without mercy. His only hope, however, is repentance toward God and faith in the Lord Jesus Christ. It is the Father's prerogative to forgive our transgressions and sins, because Christ has taken upon Himself our guilt and reprieved us, imputing to us His own righteousness. His sacrifice satisfies fully the demands of justice.

> Justification is the opposite of condemnation. God's boundless mercy is exercised toward those who are wholly undeserving. He forgives transgressions and sins for the sake of Jesus, who has become the propitiation for our sins. Through faith in Christ, the guilty transgressor is brought into favor with God and into the strong hope of life eternal.

> Strength and power have been assured to the one who comes to God admitting who they are. (Isaiah 40:28–31 ESV)

> Have you not known? Have you not heard?
> The Lord is the everlasting God, the Creator of the ends of the earth. He does not faint or grow weary; his understanding is unsearchable. He gives power to the faint, and to him who has no might he increases strength. Even youths shall faint and be weary, and young men

shall fall exhausted; but they who wait for the Lord shall renew their strength; they shall mount up with wings like eagles; they shall run and not be weary; they shall walk and not faint.

So why the preoccupation with not failing? Let's dig in further. The belief that Christians are to be perfect have long been purported by many, to their demise. Christians are to be perfect. This is the belief and expectation of many believers and nonbelievers as well. Christians are understood to be the caliber of individuals who, through some divine selection and acceptance of God's grace, through His Son, Jesus, are able to reflect the perfect character of God. Perfection is regarded as the esteemed, virtuous life that has no trace of impurity, no desire for degenerated tendencies, no cultivation of carnalities, and an indomitable hunger and thirst after righteousness. Perfection is not only the envious attraction of the one who feels degenerately deficient to stand before God; it is also the highest mark of achievement for those who will be considered eligible for glory (heaven). Let me hasten to inform you that there is biblical truth and error mixed in that explanation and expectation.

> For I can do everything through Christ, who gives me gives me strength. (Philippians 4:13 NIV)

Are Christians perfect? No! Are Christians supposed to live spiritually mature lives in Jesus Christ? Yes! So, why is imperfection still evident in the lives of Christians? Imperfection is still evident in the lives of Christians because Christians are unable to attain it, earn it, or accumulate it. Rather, Christians live under the perfect covering of Jesus Christ, the saved sinner's substitute. As simplistic as the response may sound, it is the most honest and benevolent response that can be given. The one who surrenders their life to God is given the complete perfection of Jesus Christ as a guarantee to salvation. The saved sinner's imperfections are obvious and cannot be denied, but at the same time, the saved sinner is regarded complete in God because of Jesus Christ. Pardon and justification are one and the same thing that the sinner receives from Jesus Christ. Therein lies a practical explanation of the scripture verse: "So if the Son sets you free, you will be free indeed" (John 8:36 NLT). Complete deliverance from the burden and penalty of sin.

The total cost of emancipation and amelioration is covered in the Son of God. This is good news for you and me:

> Abraham believed God, and it was counted unto him for righteousness ... Righteousness is obedience to the law. The law demands righteousness, and this the sinner owes to the law; but he is incapable of rendering it. The only way in which he can attain to righteousness is through faith. By faith he can bring to God the merits of Christ, and the Lord places the obedience of His Son to the sinner's account. Christ's righteousness is accepted in place of man's failure, and God receives, pardons, justifies, the repentant, believing soul, treats him as though he were righteous, and loves him as He loves His Son. This is how faith is accounted righteousness; and the pardoned soul goes on from grace to grace, from light to a greater light. He can say with rejoicing, "Not by works of righteousness which we have done, but according to His mercy He saved us, by the washing of regeneration, and renewing of the Holy Ghost; which He shed on us abundantly through Jesus Christ our Savior; that being justified by His grace, we should be made heirs according to the hope of eternal life. (Titus 3:5–7 AKJV)

I can understand why you would be concerned with the failures of your past. I think it is only fair that you take time to reassess your life and plan a productive future. But assessing your past as a future planning process is different from a preoccupation with the challenges that locked you in that dark time zone. There is no need to become preoccupied with spiritual failure that it becomes a personal enterprise, fought wholly on the basis of machinations to appease God and gain favor with society. By so doing, you will frustrate yourself by trying to have what you cannot give to yourself. You will also exasperate those who will not support you on your journey. Both will disappoint you. Why? God has already established a way out, and it is through the acceptance of His Son, Jesus Christ. Secondly, humanity is consistently imperfect with standards and cannot be trusted with standard settings. The goalpost is always shifting to satisfy selfish conveniences. One will never be able to satisfy the demands of our fanciful and conveniently caricatured expectations, neither can we humanly attain the standard established by God with our own strength. Both are impossibilities. What is the appropriate response to this spiritual enigma? It is total surrender of one's desires to God.

Here's another promise:

> Now unto him that is able to keep you from falling, and to present you faultless before the presence of his glory with exceeding joy, to the only wise God our Saviour, be glory and majesty, dominion and power, both now and ever. Amen. (Jude 24, 25 AKJV)

Why the fear of spiritual failure? It is fundamentally hinged to a misunderstanding of God. That misunderstanding generates a spiritual misnomer that locates God away from the journey, at the finish line, with the punishment for failing or reward for succeeding. This analogy may apply in an earthly marathon, but it wrongly fits in the Christian's journey. The one who surrenders to God has been assured divine help and support from God Himself. Bear in mind that every step you take leads you closer or farther away from a spiritually mature relationship with God. Maturity does not happen in a moment. It requires overcoming weakness after weakness. The danger is that many persons are faced with the impatience to grow, the denial of existing realities, and the projection of personal preferences of who we want others to believe we are. If only we were willing to apply faith in Jesus, our situation will change. Here's another wonderful reminder from Ellen G. White:

> Through faith, the believer passes from the position of a rebel, a child of sin and Satan, to the position of a loyal subject of Christ Jesus, not because of an inherent goodness, but because Christ receives him as His child by adoption. The sinner receives the forgiveness of his

sins, because these sins are borne by his Substitute and Surety. The Lord speaks to His heavenly Father, saying: "This is My child, I reprieve him from the condemnation of death, giving him My life insurance policy—eternal life—because I have taken his place and have suffered for his sins. He is even My beloved son." Thus man, pardoned, and clothed with the beautiful garments of Christ's righteousness, stands faultless before God.

Isaiah 41:10 (NLT) highlights that promise:

Don't be afraid, for I am with you. Don't be discouraged, for I am your God. I will strengthen you and help you. I will hold you up with my victorious right hand.

"For I am the Lord your God who takes hold of your right hand and says to you, Do not fear; I will help you. Do not be afraid, you worm Jacob, little Israel, do not fear, for I myself will help you," declares the Lord, your Redeemer, the Holy One of Israel. "See, I will make you into a threshing sledge, new and sharp, with many teeth. You will thresh the mountains and crush them, and reduce the hills to chaff." (Isaiah 41:13–15 NIV)

Fear of spiritual failure is an employment of the adversary to get us obsessed with thinking we can save ourselves. In the process, scripture is misinterpreted and meaning is misapplied. We experience distress because nothing seems to be working out for us. It is really that fear of failure is actually leading us to fail. So subtle and pervasive is that ploy that we are unable to detect it without spiritual insight.

I'm not trying to beat down on you here. It is simply that the results we have had are because of the methods we have employed to stop ourselves from failing. If you don't want to be an academic failure, applying academic principles of study—class attendance, turning in assignments on time, and showing up for examinations—are mandatory. If you don't want to be an entrepreneurial failure, then managing business funds, advertising your products, networking, and having efficient customer service and staff efficiency among other structural supports are the actions you must maintain. If you want a long-lasting relationship, commitment to your relationship values will be your motivation. If you desire to be a good parent, providing lifelong values and not just material things to your children, working alongside the other parent will be at the forefront of the relationship with your children. Using the same analogy, if you desire to be a Christian, accessing the throne room of God through prayer and Bible study is not optional; it is mandatory. There we will receive the motivations to apply spiritual principles to our lives. Only then is it possible to grow spiritually. There must be effort on your part and mine:

> Work out your own salvation with fear and trembling. (Philippians 2:12 AKJV)

> What does this mean? It means that every day you are to distrust your own human efforts and wisdom. You are to fear to speak at random, fear to follow your own impulses, fear that pride of heart and love of the world and lust of the flesh shall exclude the precious grace the Lord Jesus is longing to bestow you if you will empty the soul and make a place for it. "For it is God which worketh in you both to will and to do of his good pleasure." (Philippians 2:13 AKJV)

You must be willing to be in a position to cooperate with God. Spiritual failure becomes a reality only in the lives of those who through self-appraisals, self-praise, and self-exaltations distance themselves from the available source of all spiritual victories. The false notion that self-confidence, self-awareness, and self-reliance will stabilize and expand one's spiritual success is a major fallacy that many have fostered and regretted. Self-ambition is basically deficient and self-defeating for reliance in the spiritual journey. The journey calls for an acceptance of imperfection and a willingness to remain surrendered to God's gift of eternal life: Jesus Christ.

Here is another reminder from *Faith and Works*:

Perfection through our own good works we can never attain. The soul who sees Jesus by faith, repudiates his own righteousness. He sees himself as incomplete, his repentance insufficient, his strongest faith but feebleness, his most costly sacrifice as meager, and he sinks in humility at the foot of the cross. But a voice speaks to him from the oracles of God's Word. In amazement he hears the message, "Ye are complete in Him." Now all is at rest in his soul. No longer must he strive to find some worthiness in himself, some meritorious deed by which to gain the favor of God.

If you still have not discovered why the preoccupation with the fear of failure, let me summarize it for you. It is that the fear of failure is directly linked to an indulgence in self-sufficiency. Failure is always lurking in corners where self-adulation exists. It does not have to be that way for you. You don't have to live in failure or be afraid of failure. Why? "Jesus looked at them intently and said, 'Humanly speaking, it is impossible. But with God everything is possible'" (Matthew 19:26 NLT).

ASSESSMENT QUESTIONS

In what areas of my life am I failing?

_____

_____

In what areas of my life can I honestly say, "I've been a success"?

_____

_____

Identify four areas in your life where you have stood out as a success. Can you identify the motivations that led you to success in those areas?

_____

_____

_____

Am I motivated to grow spiritually?

_____

_____

Am I preoccupied with being perfect?

_____

_____

If I were to assess my life today, what would be my greatest joy? What makes it my greatest?

_____

_____

Using the assessment scale below, measuring from 1 to 10, record the level of satisfaction you have with your spiritual maturity:

(1) I am very dissatisfied with my spiritual maturity.
(5) I'm not so sure where I am spiritually.
(6) I am growing and motivated to do so.
(8) I am satisfied and committing to my spiritual maturity.
(10) I am very satisfied and committed to my spiritual maturity.

We should reject every tendency to portray ourselves as the ultimate example for anyone to emulate. As mannered, disciplined, schooled, economically grounded, and relationship exemplary as you may be, guard against elevating yourself as the standard bearer.

CHAPTER 7

The Fear of Sin

Spiritual immaturity equals sinful behavior, and spiritual desire plus spiritual commitment (spiritual immaturity) equals spiritual maturity.

Far too much time is spent emphasizing the adversarial nature of sin than investing in promoting the indomitable power of God's grace. The moment we begin to embrace God's desire to provide victory over our weaknesses, the less time we will spend in fear of Him.

Disclosure: I was thinking that many will decide to skip over this chapter of the book. Maybe you won't. Let's see. But if you do, I'd be elated to know the reasons. Some will find it to be spiritually liberating, and others might consider it too lenient on spiritual matters. If the latter is your position, then I have awakened the right impulse for the intended effect. I asked God to give me a liberating message for those who mistakenly miss or intentionally rebel against the spiritual mark set by Him.

The fear of sin is directly linked to fear of God. "God hates sin, and so must I. If I don't hate sin, then I am not united with God in obedience and character." If this is the conclusion of the whole matter, then surely this calls for a reassessment of your commitment to spirituality, especially in your devotional life. Why? Time spent with God will positively impact the heart of the willing soul to a deeper spiritual union. However, if you live in fear of God because of your knowledge of His hatred for sin, there is an immediate need to intensify the desire to know God.

The fear of sin speaks to a deeper consciousness of God and the desire to please Him who knows no sin. His only begotten Son lived in human flesh and was in all points tempted as we are, yet He did not sin (Hebrews

4:15 AKJV). Make no mistake in your understanding of what should be the desire of the one who wants to walk with God. Provision has been made for all today, which was expressed for the salvation of all who would accept Him as the anointed Messiah:

> But as many as received him, to them gave he power to become the sons of God, even to them that believe on his name. (John 1:12 AKJV)

It is not the absence of provision that mulls the desire to walk with God. Lets be clear on that. Rather, the expectation of perfection fuels fear of God in the sinner.

The struggle to accept imperfection as a natural part of our existence is very real. This is completely different from expressing desire to live imperfectly, while reluctant to accept that we live with inherent imperfection and should not hate who we are. Herein lies the challenge for imperfect humankind. The difficulty in the expectation is that the one who is to accept and promote perfection is imperfect and does not have the innate capacity to produce perfection. The attainment, consequently, remains an illusion for the unconverted. Like fantasy, it fills the atmosphere and carpets the barren ground, but at nightfall, it bows away and fades into the sunset only to be repeated again and again. Perfection remains that reality that can only be truly understood within the context of divinity. This is the source of all fear for the one striving to live righteously.

Let's detail some of the scenarios and beliefs linked to fear of sin on the journey with God.

1. **The fear of being outside of God's favor is unsettling for believers, nonbelievers, and apostates.** Have you ever prayed and subsequently felt inspired by the power of God in your life—to the point that you want to remember the day, the time, and the circumstances that motivated you to pray that prayer? Don't you want to remember the exact words of that prayer so you can pray it again and again. Don't you want the inspiration that you received the first time you prayed those words? Did you know that both the believing and the nonbelieving believe they should believe in a power that is supreme? Even when it is disturbing for the nonbelieving

to agree on who that power is or may be, there is this acceptance that I am aware of a consciousness that I cannot explain but know is real. The believers acknowledge God's power to structure and to lead their lives. The nonbelievers, on the other hand, are uncertain that God is able to efficiently and sufficiently take them through their journey, therefore making no allowance for His company. The believing begin the journey with God and do not want to jeopardize that relationship at any cost to their eternal reward. The nonbelievers, though noncommittally desirous of receiving God's mercies, remain aware of His involvement in the universe and the affairs of this world. Hence the spiritual struggle in the hearts of all humankind: to accept or to reject God.

2. **The fear of losing God's presence and power is frightening to both believers and nonbelievers.** The Christian wrestles with the reality at a relationship depth rather than at the platonic level. The Christian seeks to answer the question: "How can I remain faithful to the choice that I have made to walk with God?" The non-Christian battles the desire to accept the saving grace of God or deny the need for it, thereby continuing to live outside of His salvation.

Fear of losing God's presence and power in my life has propelled me to my knees with such irresistible motivation that I thank God for the time and place it happened. The desire to be right with God was and remains at war with the desire to satisfy pleasurable desires. In Freud's psychoanalytic theory of personality, there is a constant force exerted by the id for immediate gratification of all urges, wants, and needs. It's referred to as the pleasure principle. That force strives to fulfill our most basic and primitive urges, including hunger, thirst, anger, and sex. When these needs are not met, the result is a state of anxiety or tension. The management of such demands is done by the reality principle called the ego. Let's apply those principles to the Christian experience.

The Christian and the non-Christian experiences the struggle between the id and the ego (pleasure principle versus the reality principle). In writing to Romans converted to Christianity, the apostle Paul provided the liberating acceptance of the struggle against the denial of Christians who would prefer to deny the compelling power of desire (Romans 7 AKJV). This is not to establish desire above the power of choice. In no way! It is to establish that denying the power of desire is to deprive oneself of much-needed acknowledgment for greater life victories. The first victory is to accept that desires are not inherently evil. The second is to accept that humankind desires good as well as evil. Humankind desires community as much as they desire isolation in times of adversity. Humankind desires wealth, which gives access to comfortable community living. The third victory is to accept the unwillingness on the part of human beings to choose the less pleasurable option. Humankind contends with the lack of courage to deny themselves whatever they desire even at the cost of potential dangers to self and to society.

3. **Many Christians do not feel liberated from their pasts and therefore cannot enjoy their journeys with God.** Letting go of past memories is not easily done as is often expected. Believers as well as nonbelievers form attachments, and those attachments impact every facet of their lives, negatively or positively so. Plainly said, many are hooked to the past and genuinely struggle to let go. As appealing as the journey ahead may seem, fond memories of the past sometimes seem equally appealing and irresistible to cherish. Severing ties with the past seems overwhelmingly difficult because attachments provide psychological benefits. Attachments reflect the times and situations that engendered those past experiences. Many feel that if they let go of those memories, they would, inadvertently, be giving up on past agreements, endearing friendships, and long-held convictions. As a result, the past is always standing up to them and asking for a place in their future. Guilt and shame motivate many to despair and lose hope in all possible future changes. The grace of God seems too good to be true and is therefore rejected.

The one who accepts the invitation to walk with God must be willing to accept the past and not try to deny it. Acceptance of a sordid past is just as important to your future spiritual, social, psychological, and financial development as acceptance of an academic degree for your future career. It's yours. You have to own it. You may not always be proud of it. That's understandably justifiable! Do not deny its inscription on the walls of your life. Identify with the lessons learned, the troubled waters, the kindled fires, the missteps and mishaps, and the intentional and unintentional behaviors, but never ignore the call to own your past.

4. **The fear of not being good enough for God grips the hearts of many developing Christians.**

Sadly, the developing Christian often loses sight of God and develops a preoccupation with being perfect in the sight of others. Their gaze would be set on those, who like them, stand deficient before God, outside of His grace. The gaze would be so rigidly locked to like humans that the behavior of the supposedly faithful would influence the behaviors of the not so faithful.

The tendency to earn and display one's qualifications for salvation only dwarfs the spiritual development of many would-be spiritual giants. The fear of not being good enough for God must be surrendered to Him, who alone is able to work on the heart and produce a character that will far exceed the expectations of those around us. Too many times, we give leverage to our pasts and deprive all possibilities of growth in our future. For too long, you have been handing those keys to an interest that is not supportive of you. Fear of not being good enough for God is all the adversary needs to manipulate your life and reconstruct your conscience from being hopeful to disparaging.

What you need to do is change the locks on those doors. Don't bother to ask your enemy to return the keys. You can do without them. There is a more comprehensive protection plan to benefit your future. Bear in mind that human deficiencies, despite the degree to which they occupied the history of the repentant, have no power to stall the surrendered walk with God. The walk begins with God's full acceptance of our past and full acknowledgment of all possible future spiritual deviations, mistakenly or deliberately so.

God, however, has made allowance for all possible human ineptitude along the way:

> My dear children, I am writing this to you so that you will not sin. But if anyone does sin, we have an advocate who pleads our case before the Father. He is Jesus Christ, the one who is truly righteous. (1 John 2:1 NIV)

> Where sin abounded, grace did much more abound. (Romans 5:20 AKJV)

> The Christian is not immune to inner spiritual conflicts.
> Romans 7:14 (NRSV) clearly enunciates the struggle for
> every spiritual sojourner: "For we know that the law is
> spiritual; but I am of the flesh, sold into slavery under sin."

The struggle is real for the Christian as the non-Christian. The
Christian wrestles with the desire to desire what is undesirable for spiritual
development and consecrated living. The Christian remains aware of the
existing and compelling power of such desires even as effort is made to get
to their destination. Despite the efforts, the tendency to deviate from the
path may be satisfied once, twice, thrice, four times, five times, six times,
and more times than ever anticipated:

> So I am not the one doing wrong; it is sin living in me that
> does it. And I know that nothing good lives in me, that
> is, in my sinful nature. I want to do what is right, but I
> can't. I want to do what is good, but I don't. I don't want
> to do what is wrong, but I do it anyway. But if I do what
> I don't want to do, I am not really the one doing wrong;
> it is sin living in me that does it. (Romans 7:17–20 NLT)

It is an opportune time to debunk the highly sensationalized religious
phrase "God of a second chance." I have commented umpteenth times in
biblical lectures and sermons that it may be religiously captivating to say,
"God is the God of a second chance," but it sure is theologically misleading
to make that pronouncement. Why? Because you and I are well aware that
we messed up our second chances a long time ago:

> I do not understand my own actions. For I do not do
> what I want, but I do the very thing I hate. (Romans 7:15
> NRSV)

The issue for the believer is not the absence of dissonance from what is
desired. Make no mistake about it. There is knowledge that the disconnect
exists. There is awareness of an unnatural presence empowering the heart's
natural desire.

> For I know that nothing good dwells within me, that is, in
> my flesh. I can will what is right, but I cannot do it. For
> I do not do the good I want, but the evil I do not want is
> what I do. (Romans 7:18, 19 NRSV)

The heart self-servingly acknowledges that compelling desire that more often than not is mirrored to appear more attractive than the alternative. It is through submission to the transformative power of God that victory is attained in this conflict.

Knowledge of imperfections or awareness of need does not automatically translate into activation of transformative desires. On the contrary, at the moment there is recognition of deficiencies in your walk with God, the spiritual struggle intensifies. The intensification suddenly becomes more troubling because you now need to decide what your next course of action will be. Will I discontinue my journey and return to my previous recognition of who I was—or do I continue the trek, fully cognizant that I will triumph even if it means breaking through significant barriers? This will become the language of spiritual survival over mere spiritual profession and comfort.

5. **The believer must come to terms with human imperfection.** Imperfections need to be seen as a by-product of sin. Sin needs to be understood as a direct consequence of humankind's sinful nature and willful disobedience of God's divine instruction. God's directives are perfectly wholesome and rewarding. David renders God's acknowledgment of humankind:

> God looks down from heaven on all humankind to see if
> there are any who understand, any who seek God; Everyone
> has turned away, all have become corrupt; there is no one
> who does good, not even one. (Psalm 53:2, 3 NIV)

Just the thought of acknowledging imperfection disturbs the fascination of the fanatic with perfection. Some think it should not be part of the believer's spiritual acceptance and that imperfection fuels imperfection and must not be an accepted reality in the life of the believer. Needless to say, there is grave danger in that position.

6. **Believers and nonbelievers are similarly imperfect.** Both have a proclivity for sinful pleasures, both experience inner spiritual conflicts, and both need spiritual advocacy for all of their journeys with God:

> There is no one righteous, not even one; there is no one who understands; there is no one who seeks God. All have turned away, they have together become worthless; there is no one who does good, not even one. (Romans 3:10–12 NIV)

The earlier the believer accepts this spiritual reality, the more enriching their walk with God will be.

Would you mind doing some calculations with me? Better yet, on your own:

> Perhaps you have sinned once for every day you have lived.
> Multiply that by the number of days in a regular month.
> Multiply by the number of months in a year.
> Multiply that by the number of years you have lived.

Allow me to engage you further in asking the following questions while stirring your salvation interests:

> What was your calculation?
> How many times have you sinned in your lifetime?
> How many chances at being perfect have you receive?
> Have many opportunities at becoming perfect did you not improve?
> How do you intend to remedy that situation?
> Can you get back those opportunities to give a better report of yourself? How so?

Romans 6:14–22 (AKJV) provides a basis for my personal reflection on the believer's struggle to disassociate with imperfection.

Personal Reflections on Spiritual Freedom

Sin no longer has jurisdiction over you. The law with its demands can no longer force you to live under its requirements. Instead, you now live in covenant under the freedom of God's grace.

Since God's grace has freed us from the enslavement of the law, does that mean we are at liberty to practice sinning? Of course not! Haven't you realized that you are in servitude of whatever you choose to obey? You can live in bondage with sin, resulting in eternal death—or you can choose to live in obedience to God, which results in eternal living. Thank God! You ought to rejoice! You were living in servitude to sin before now, but since you accepted the teachings we gave you, you are now living a life of commitment to God. Your enslavement is no longer to sin but to righteous living.

Be aware that I am using the analogy of slavery to help you understand the principle of liberty because of the infirmities of your human nature. Before now, you permitted yourselves to be slaves to impurity and lawlessness, which only led you so much deeper into sin. Now, I urge you to give yourselves as slaves to righteous living so you can enjoy holiness, the benefits of liberation from sinful bondage.

When you were slaves to sin, you could not have satisfied any of the obligations for righteous living. You had no liberty. And what was the result? Now, you are ashamed of your past actions—even those things that have eternal consequences. That was then. It is not so anymore since you are free from the power of sin and have become slaves of God. Now your life is actively filled with those things that lead to holiness and result in eternal life.

7. **It is perfectly normal to accept that humanity is imperfect and prone to making mistakes.** It is not sinful to accept imperfection as a human condition. Accepting that reality qualifies you for the abundant grace of God. David acknowledged the genesis of his silent and open spiritual battles, and it would be wise for you to note your silent and or open spiritual battles:

It is perfectly normal to own your imperfection. Imperfection says, "I need trans-formation."

But I was born a sinner, yes, from the moment my mother conceived me. (Psalm 51:5 TLB)

Surely I was sinful at birth, sinful from the time my mother conceived me. (Psalm 51:5 NIV)

The apostle Paul alerted his converts of the enormity of all humankind's struggles:

For all have sinned and fall short of the glory of God. (Romans 3:23 NIV)

Therefore, just as sin entered the world through one man, and death through sin, and in this way death came to all people, because all sinned— To be sure, sin was in the world before the law was given, but sin is not charged against anyone's account where there is no law. Nevertheless, death reigned from the time of Adam to the time of Moses, even over those who did not sin by breaking a command, as did Adam, who is a pattern of the one to come. (Romans 5:12–14 NIV)

8. Adam, the symbol of man's origin, the first, the beginning of all human creation, is also the genesis representation of death.

That death, physical and spiritual, has now been passed to all generations. Adam's legacy to all other generations is death because of his willful disobedience on his journey with his Creator. The only escape from that degenerative curse is to accept the perfection of the second Adam, that humankind again can experience incorruption:

> For as in Adam all die, even so in Christ shall all be made alive. (1 Corinthians 15:22 NIV)

Incorruption and immortality are found within the gift of salvation. The gift of salvation in Jesus Christ is complete redemption from a degenerated life. How does this happen? When saved sinners tell the stories of how their lives were regenerated, other sinners will believe them and will act upon their belief:

> Whoever believes and is baptized will be saved, but whoever does not believe will be condemned. (Mark 16:16 NIV)

9. Baptism into the Lord Jesus Christ does not provide immunity from sinful tendencies or provide anyone with incorruptible flesh. Rather, confession of sins followed by repentance of a contrary lifestyle for the perfect character of Jesus Christ and His saving grace is demonstrated through the public rite of water baptism by immersion. This experience, though it does not inoculate anyone from temptation, including lust and idolatry, guarantees the sinner immediate salvation.

The believer's commitment to that salvation experience is only demonstrable in walking with God. That walk exposes the saved sinner to the much-needed transformation in their character as they are daily exposed to the character of Jesus Christ, the only constant goalpost and standard of godlikeness. He is God's gift of salvation to you and every other sinner. Stop trying to measure up to those who, like you, need to accept their imperfections. Stop grieving over expressed imperfections and pay attention to the provisions of your salvation. Recognize that all you do will forever remain inadequate to give you sufficient credibility to measure up to the perfect character of God. Jesus Christ is your substitute. I am not yours—and you are not mine.

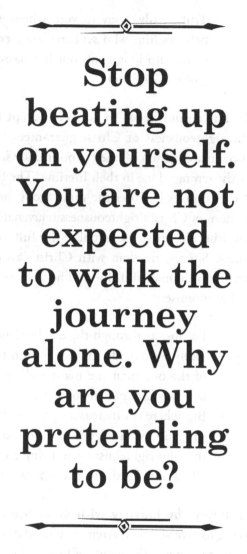

Stop beating up on yourself. You are not expected to walk the journey alone. Why are you pretending to be?

10. **Salvation is guaranteed as a free gift from God.** Salvation is rendered to the sinner as an eternal gift. The sinner must continue to believe in the gift of salvation to receive the benefits of the gift of salvation:

> But the person who endures to the end will be saved. (Matthew 24:13 ESV)

The demonstration of the sinner's belief is in the lifestyle since the conviction is in the heart. The demonstrative work is the work of a lifetime. For the journey of a lifetime, the saved sinner is guaranteed the company of God.

> Truly, truly, I say to you, whoever hears my word and believes him who sent me has eternal life. He does not come into judgment, but has passed from death to life. (John 5:24 ESV)

11. The sinner needs to actively accept the righteousness of Christ. The righteousness of Christ guarantees freedom. That freedom is an absolute abrogation of one's exposure to God's wrath and final judgment for the wrongs done in their lifetime. The freedom that the righteousness of Christ gives liberates the mind from the guilt and shame of sin. The freedom of Christ's righteousness rejuvenates the psyche of the guilty and unleashes the innate potential to live fully and happily with self and with others. Simply, freedom with Christ cancels the debt owed to the law because of human sinfulness. The apostle Paul established the certainty of that promise:

> For just as through the disobedience of the one man the many were made sinners, so also through the obedience of the one man the many will be made righteous. The law was brought in so that the trespass might increase. But where sin increased, grace increased all the more, so that, just as sin reigned in death, so also grace might reign through righteousness to bring eternal life through Jesus Christ our Lord. (Romans 5:19–21 NIV)

12. Enjoy the journey with God. Stop condemning yourself. Stop trying to save yourself. Aren't you tired of the frustration that comes with trying to appease the wrath of God, which can only be satisfied through the acceptance of His Son, Jesus Christ? No amount of rituals will qualify you for salvation. Your human efforts without the active grace of God will bring to you what hopelessness and despair result in the depressed individual. Embrace the promise that:

> Therefore, there is now no condemnation for those who are in Christ Jesus, because through Christ Jesus the law of the Spirit who gives life has set you free from the law of sin and death. (Romans 8:1–2 NIV)

Let there be conviction between your actions and your words. Words plus action express commitment. There is no standalone experience. Spiritual disconnection will look impressive on the walls of make believe, but it will cloud the windows of conviction. I say, accept the promise and power of eternal salvation in your life. "So if the Son sets you free, you will be free indeed" (John 8:36 NIV). You will not benefit from your spiritual potential until you wholeheartedly accept the gift of salvation. What will it be for you?

13. **Learn to communicate in the language of salvation and not the language of self-exaltation.** The repentant sinner who comes to God through His Son, Jesus Christ early recognizes that nothing but the language of gratitude, respect, adoration, commitment, and exaltation (grace) of God is acceptable on your journey with Him. The repentant will early realize that companionship with God demands less focus on self and more on God. In a very specific manner, the repentant accepts grace as unmerited favor explicitly given for salvation. This is the only principle that will provide spiritual support to the relationship.

Sinful behavior is an expression of existing spiritual immaturity.

Self must be given second place. Self-worship, self-aggrandizement, self-pity, and self-pride must abdicate the throne. Nothing less than sincere worship from a broken and contrite heart will be acceptable to God. When this is readily done, the spiritual journey transforms from fear to friendship. Trust in God becomes more evident in the lifestyle and bears fruit for greater service. Worship becomes exciting and humility becomes practical.

The prophet Amos emphasizes that principle when he asked, "For how can we walk together with your sins between us?" (Amos 3:3 TLB). Another version says, "Do two walk together unless they have agreed to do so?" (Amos 3:3 NIV). It is important to recognize that the entire universe is in God's care, yet particular undistorted attention is being given to you to ensure you reach your destination. This is a testament of His love for you, His identification with your realities, His acknowledgment of your needs, and His commitment to a more meaningful relationship with Him.

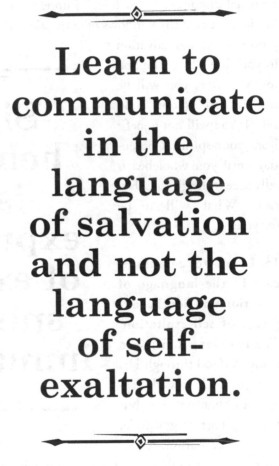

Learn to communicate in the language of salvation and not the language of self-exaltation.

14. **The language of salvation is a language of overcoming and not a boast of having arrived.** The soul-searching believer recognizes that self-acclaimed victories are magnetic opportunities for self-destruction. Not

that there would not be opportunities self-exaltation. Such moments will frequently show up and show off their intentions.

It is flattering to highlight the misgivings that are evident in the lives of others and a nonissue in ours. For example, he smokes, but I don't. She works on Sabbath, but I don't. He drinks, but I don't. She's worldly, but I'm not. He is divorced, but I'm not. He's gay, but I'm not. He's an abuser, but I'm not. He has tattoos, but I don't. It is so easy to pull out the drawer of religiosity and find the exact labels, we believe, that are suitable for others even when our conscience is calling loudly to pay attention to who we are. How charming and consoling it is to the deceptive heart to constructively dismiss self-exaltation as a sin and look with disdain upon others who display physical evidence of differences and spiritual immaturity.

I have discovered that deception lies comfortably on the inside of those who have no compunction for the salvation of souls. Their preoccupation with themselves is tied to selfishness, conceit, and self-worship.

The maturing believer acknowledges the emphasis of the scriptures to live a spiritually mature life. It is a goal that mandates a commitment to feed from the Word of God. It is in the Word of God that a searching soul finds needed guidance for spiritual development. The Word teaches that maturity, though gradual, results in spiritual empowerment over natural sinful tendencies (1 John 3:7–9 NLT):

> Dear children, don't let anyone deceive you about this: When people do what is right, it shows that they are righteous, even as Christ is righteous. But when people keep on sinning, it shows that they belong to the devil, who has been sinning since the beginning. But the Son of God came to destroy the works of the devil.
>
> Those who have been born into God's family do not make a practice of sinning because God's life is in them. So, they can't keep on sinning because they are children of God.

What then is the course of action for the spiritual sojourner? When under the tempter's grip, the heart feels compelled to satisfy natural compulsions. It is therefore unsafe to say, "Because I am a Christian, all that comes to my mind to do has been placed there by God."

The enemy of the soul will engage the senses and activate the sinful traits encrypted in your DNA, motivating even the experienced believer away from their destination. Spiritual tenacity, therefore, does not exist in mere words but in the divine activation of the will to apply the Word of God to the heart. Words applied to the heart will translate to actions in the life of the one who desires transformation. How does this happen? Transformation takes place in the patiently committed heart and demonstrated through the behaviors of the consecrated life.

Prayer

Dear God, I ask you for greater faith: faith to take me beyond where I now stand, faith to fortify me in times of adversities and difficulties like now. Give me the fortitude to hold on, the resilience to press on, and the courage to withstand the attacks of the adversary. Give me the hope, heavenly Father, that all will be well between me and You. Give to me a greater desire for Your Word and the desire to accept the power of Your Word in my life. In Jesus's name, I pray. Amen! Amen! Amen!

ASSESSMENT QUESTIONS

What is/are my inner spiritual conflict/s?

_____

_____

Am I a confident believer or am I afraid to acknowledge my spiritual strengths?

_____

_____

How do I know that I am maturing spiritually?

_____

_____

Have I learned to communicate in the language of salvation and not in the language of self-exaltation?

_____

_____

Am I uncomfortable in knowing that I am imperfect?

_____

_____

How does being imperfect influence my view of others?

_____

_____

Am I giving leverage to my past, hanging on to my imperfections, and stifling my future? In what way/s?

_____

_____

What is contributing to my spiritual immaturity?

_____

_____

CHAPTER 3

Grace Is the Language of Salvation

Gratitude for God

Respect (Reverence) for God

Adoration for God

Commitment to God

Exaltation of God in practical worship

CHAPTER 8

A Favorite of Mine

Stand up, take up your bed, and walk!
—John 5: 1–15 (AKJV)

Here are some indisputable facts:

No one wants to be or enjoys being sick.
No one wants to be incapacitated by any circumstance, particularly in the most productive years of their life.
Everyone wants their dreams to materialize within record-breaking time—if not immediately.
Everyone wants total recovery from any illness.
Everyone wants to be mentally healthy for as long as they live.
Everyone anticipates some degree of fairness and cooperation from others—even when interfacing with strangers.
Everyone believes that the worst days of their lives will remain distant and possibly never be realized.
Everyone wants a formidable recovery plan when anticipations go off script in life.

This conundrum is illustrated in the narrative of John 5: 1–15 (AKJV).

What you are about to read is a transgenerational, intercontinental, interracial, interfaith, and classic description of real-life circumstances faced by all classes of real people in various stages of their lives.

Jesus transacted a miracle on the seventh-day Sabbath:

> Afterward Jesus returned to Jerusalem for one of the Jewish holy days.
>
> Inside the city, near the Sheep Gate, was the pool of Bethesda, with five covered porches.
>
> Crowds of sick people—blind, lame, or paralyzed—lay on the porches.
>
> One of the men lying there had been sick for thirty-eight years.
>
> When Jesus saw him and knew he had been ill for a long time, he asked him,
>
> "Would you like to get well?"
>
> I can't, sir," the sick man said, "for I have no one to put me into the pool when
>
> the water bubbles up. Someone else always gets there ahead of me."
>
> Jesus told him, "Stand up, pick up your mat, and walk!"
>
> Instantly, the man was healed! He rolled up his sleeping mat and began walking!
>
> But this miracle happened on the Sabbath, so the Jewish leaders objected. They said to the man who was cured, "You can't work on the Sabbath! The law doesn't allow you to carry that sleeping mat!" But he replied, "The man who healed me told me, 'Pick up your mat and walk.'
>
> "Who said such a thing as that?" they demanded.
>
> The man didn't know, for Jesus had disappeared into the crowd.
>
> But afterward Jesus found him in the Temple and told him, "Now you are well; so stop sinning, or something even worse may happen to you."
>
> Then the man went and told the Jewish leaders that it was Jesus who had healed him.
>
> (John 5:1–15 NLT)

Discussion

A certain man was surrounded by many other sick people. According to the narration, his age is unknown, his societal status unrecognized, and social standing undetermined. We have no idea of the distance from which the impotent man traveled to be at the poolside. The pool had five porches, but we do not have any knowledge of the porch where he may have first been located.

We don't know if impotence was the only motivation for him being at the poolside or that societal rejection by pseudo friends, ungrateful relatives, or unforgiving neighbors granted him eligible candidacy for poolside existence. Further, we don't know how many persons were at the poolside before him, the severity of the illnesses of those whom he met there, or even those who came after his arrival.

What seems very evident from the account is that the scenery was colored with sickness instead of happiness and that the impotent male, as was his poolside neighbors, was expecting to be healed of his disease through a miraculous maneuvering of the water at an unspecified time of day. The time for the moving of the water was unspecified, and the uncertainty of getting into the water for the healing that they all anticipated so much.

One may reasonably conclude that he may have gotten closer to the miracle pool with every passing day. At least his exchange with Jesus seems to suggest that he would have intentionally tried to get into the pool—only to be overtaken by other capable sick poolside neighbors:

> When Jesus saw him and knew he had been ill for a long time, he asked him, 'Would you like to get well?'
> "I can't, sir," the sick man said, "for I have no one to put me into the pool when the water bubbles up. Someone else always gets there ahead of me." (John 5:6, 7 NLT)

The usual atmosphere was changed when Jesus got to the scene and began His interrogation of one of the poolside residents. Skipping the details of how they were introduced, and Jesus's knowledge of the severity and duration of his illness, Jesus asked the question that still reverberates in the heart of every socially, mentally, physically, economically, and spiritually challenged individual today: "Do you want to be made well?" (John 5:6 NKJV). The question reflects contextual inappropriateness and situational insensitivity, and it has a confrontational approach.

"Do you want to be made well?" Was Jesus not aware of his surroundings? How long has he been there to see the attempts by the poolside occupants to get closer to or inside the miracle pool? Since you know the circumstances surrounding the person of your choice, why ask the question?

Can't you see that I am unwell? the sick man may have thought. *This is not the time to be asking me such a question. You are looking at me. Are you interested in helping me out or not? For goodness's sake, do something about my situation. If you can ask the question, it may be that you can do something about my condition. Are you going to relieve me of my distress—or are you asking only to walk away like other spectators have done before?*

These are just some of the reasonable questions that the sick man could have asked at the time Jesus confronted him. Make no mistake about his reasoning. There was no limit to which his mind could have traveled because there was no reason why he did not want to get well and walk away from that poolside. The man's situation was hopeless at his previous location. There, at the poolside, he had acted on the many stories told about the miracle pool. There was an immediate resonating response to the question of Jesus. The sick man would wait no longer to confront his situation with the question asked by the stranger who happens to be the Son of God. His patience had run out and no longer allowed him to stay in that place. No more was he willing to use explanations, though legitimate, to keep him from having a productive life. The moment for which he had long waited seemed all so real before, but something was different about this time. Something was different about the stranger and the connection they had:

> The impotent man answered him, "Sir, I have no man, when the water is troubled, to put me into the pool: but while I am coming, another steppeth down before me." (John 5:7 KJV)

> "I can't," the sick man said, "for I have no one to help me into the pool at the movement of the water. While I am trying to get there, someone else always gets in ahead of me." (John 5:7 TLB)

> The sick man answered him, "Sir, I have no one to put me into the pool when the water is stirred up. While I am trying to get into the water, someone else goes down there before me." (John 5:7 NET)

From all indications, the sick man recognized that his many past unsuccessful attempts at getting into the pool were indicative of future unsuccessful attempts for a changed life. He laid claim to the authority that the stranger exuded. Without reservation, he put his entire future into the hands of a complete stranger. He specifically spoke to his physical condition (inability to get into the water), his desire (waiting for the moving of the water to get in), his dream (someone to get him in the water), and his hope (getting healed). What an unfortunate place to be.

The sick man appealed to the conscience of Jesus in his response. He was asking the stranger to be different and assist him in getting to the water. He was asking the stranger to exercise compassion in the midst of desperation that was evident around the poolside. He petitioned the courage of the stranger to both demonstrate interest and hospitality to a dreamer among other desperate dreamers.

Anguish had reached its zenith. From the lips of hopelessness could have been heard these words: "Let me have the opportunity of a lifetime. Please, I'm begging you. I need it!" Impotence was relentlessly pursuing healing. The man had gotten tired of staying at the poolside. Let me point out a lesson in the attitude displayed by the impatient man: Don't teach yourself to accept what's not good for you. Further, don't romanticize deficiency, ineptitude, evil, or illness—even when discomfort looms at your door.

> The sick man answered him, "Sir, I have no one to put me into the pool when the water is stirred up. While I am trying to get into the water, someone else goes down there before me." (John 5:7 NET)

The despairing cry of the sick man is the cry of many today: the inability to achieve that documented dream, inaccessibility to those necessary resources, lack of encouragement from those who ought to be meaning more, the absence of romantic affirmations, the overwhelming tone of criticism over the comforting voice of care, the loudness of dissenting voices over the empowering voices of hope and support, the loud fragrance of demoralization over the delinquent presence of collegiality, the deafening silence of long-term friendships over the tensions of developing acquaintances, the occupation of invading forces in once friendly and confiding territories, and the emotional disconnections even in regimented physical presence. The cries of anguish over the symphony of hope. In the midst of all of those present, none qualified, by their own doing and own situation, to assist the other into the miracle pool.

Personal dreams were wrapped up in immense poolside desperation. Though everyone there was sick, they all believed that the pool offered seasons of healing and that it was preceded by an angel stirring the water. As often as the water was stirred, a dream was realized. That's the level of commitment each sick individual had at the poolside.

Evident in this illustration is the need for us today to be committed to our dreams. Fear of someone getting ahead of us should only serve to energize our determination to achieve. Getting ahead of the line does not always result in getting the best. It is not always true that the early bird catches the best worm. Preparation to catch the best worm gives you the opportunity to know the best worm. So, prepare to catch the best worm.

> The fastest runner doesn't always win the race, and the strongest warrior doesn't always win the battle. The wise sometimes go hungry, and the skillful are not necessarily wealthy. And those who are educated don't always lead successful lives. It is all decided by chance, by being in the right place at the right time. People can never predict when hard times might come. Like fish in a net or birds in a trap, people are caught by sudden tragedy. (Proverbs 9:11, 12 NLT)

Speed without preparation often results in unprecedented failure. Failure forms friendships only with those who are unsuspecting of its agenda.

In your walk with God, the presence of others around you does not naturally translate into the convenience of hospitality. This was illustrated in the narrative under consideration. Those around you may not have the capacity to provide the level of assistance that you need. On the contrary, they may, for the survival of their agenda, need to disassociate with you or you with them. Disassociation with like incapacitated individuals is an asset to all concern. Everyone gets to reassess and modify their dreams where necessary. Disassociation is not synonymous with hate, and it does not translate to indifference. Dissociation means that our agendas are different and consequently deserve appropriate approaches in order to achieve the anticipated goal. The prophet Amos asked, "Can two people walk together without agreeing on the direction?" Amos 3:3 (NLT). No!

The sick man's fear was short-lived. The heart of Jesus recognized the potential lying on the mat at the poolside. His eyes pierced through the corridors of time and realized the impact of that man's life to succeeding generations. As Jesus gazed into the eyes of impotence, His earthly mission was reaffirmed. He was moved with the soul of compassion, by the hands of justice, with the courage of emancipation, and with unselfish zeal for the soul of the man He had just met. Not for one moment more would He allow impotence to lock the jaw of potential and disability to shackle the hands of the future. Jesus saw hope and redemption while impotence was fighting to hold onto its undeserved victim. Instead of highlighting and discussing the circumstances that may have led to the man's illness, Jesus, in divine authority, broke the chains that kept him impotent.

"Take up your bed and walk" (John 5:8 AKJV) was the instruction given. No other words for the salvation of the soul of that man could have been spoken. No better time could it have been given than then. Although the situation existed long before Jesus arrived on the scene, the hunger for the much-desired change was heightened when the question was asked: "Do you want to be made well?" (John 5:6 NKJV). No other being could have spoken directly to the problem than Jesus. By instructing the man to take up his bed and walk, Jesus transformed his reality, canceled all future plans to be at the poolside, and gave him inspiration for a fulfilling tomorrow.

"Take up your bed and walk" (John 5:8 AKJV), spoken from the lips of humankind's Redeemer was without partiality and conditionality. No restriction was then placed on the possibility of the man's restoration. He was given all rights and privileges by the authority of heaven, as prescribed by Jesus, Mary's baby, Immanuel, the only begotten Son of God, and in testimony whereof the powers of the Trinity are affixed.

"Take up your bed and walk" (John 5:8 AKJV) was a commandment spoken for the complete transformation of the man's life, for the cancellation of his past, and a rebuke to anything that may seek to redirect his future. No longer did he have to explain his limitations to get to the pool to be healed. He did not again need physical healing. The man's need was spiritual healing. He no longer had to worry about the stirring of the water "at some time of the day."

In a very instructive way, "Take up your bed and walk" (John 5:8 AKJV) is a clarion call for disadvantaged, marginalized people, widows, and widowers to relocate from the pseudo comforts of organizational structures that do nothing to help them heal from their protracted illnesses. Instead of creating access to the pool that is sufficient for all to survive, for the sick ones to get healed, many societal structures promote dogged individualism that stirs the water of unfair competition for the disadvantaged. Those structures dangle opportunities for economic growth, better health care, modern social safety nets, and educational opportunities, but those opportunities remain inaccessible because of inflexible regulations and systemic discriminations. The emancipation call is to get out of the accustomed zone that has been made popular by your incapacities, your ignorance, your fears, and your dependencies. You have been living on promissory notes that remain

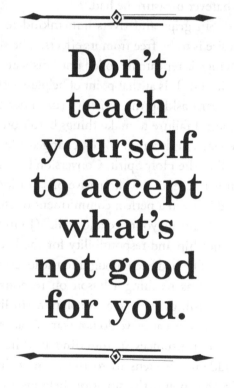

Don't teach yourself to accept what's not good for you.

non-cashable even if they bear overdue maturity dates. Those promissory notes have been devalued by the lack of committed signatories for fear that they themselves will be incapacitated by a dishonorable society.

"Take up your bed and walk" (John 5:8 AKJV) established three principles linked to the spiritual doctrine of righteousness by faith. Firstly, let us recognize the incapacitation of the man and his neighbors at the poolside. They had much in common but were different at the core. The man symbolized sinners wanting to change their lives but incapacitated to do so. Innumerable attempts would be made to no avail. Secondly, he surrendered his desire for healing to the one whom he accepted to have the capacity to heal him. Thirdly, the impotent man exercised his faith, whatever measure he had.

Sin grips and rivets humankind to their challenges even when the desire is to be free from its effects. The shameful cry of failed attempts to change is repeatedly soiled until disheartenment renders it ineffective and pointless. It is at that point of helplessness that the voice of the Holy Spirit is heard asking the sinner to surrender to Jesus what has already been a colossal failure to make things better on their own. The sinner confesses, repents, and commits to a changed life through the surrendering of the will to the Holy Spirit. Conversion begins at the station of surrender. The sinner accepts the alternative of salvation by grace through faith in Jesus and is given a perfect commitment of eternal life in God.

"Take up your bed and walk" (John 5:8 AKJV) also established direct ownership and responsibility for the bed to the sick man. It was his bed even if he had been brought to the location by a friendly or unkind person. Jesus was teaching a lesson on responsibility and choice. Many times, when things don't go as we plan in our lives, it is easier to point a finger at someone because we do not want to accept responsibility for the situation or circumstances surrounding it. The reality of being at the poolside suddenly awakens us to the grim reality of choices and consequences. At that point, the situation belongs to a person who, in our distressed estimation, volunteered to be our persecutor, our nemesis, or the grim reaper of our soul. At such times, we need to introspectively identify the decisions that brought us to the poolside.

I am by no means suggesting that we may not, inadvertently, be confronted with mishaps along the journey to triumphant living.

Misadventure will occur to our disagreements. Yes! I am, however, identifying the need to own those laissez-faire attitudes that land us in financial distress, unimproved opportunities that disadvantage our potential, procrastinations that lead to failing grades, abusiveness that favors separation or divorce for the protection of life, persistent infidelities that lead to divorce, unforgiving attitudes that transform cherished relationships into bedrocks of regret, irrational decisions that birth imprisonments, intemperance that leads to drunkenness, overconfidence that leads to unwanted pregnancies, rebellious friendships that lead to drug addictions, faithlessness that stirs anxieties, fanaticism that fundamentally shatters meaningful spiritual growth, conceitedness that births paranoia, obsessions that trigger psychoses, greed that fosters illegalities, impulsiveness that leads to incompatible marriages, jealousies that usher unreasonable vexations, and anger that broods resentments. The bed has an owner, and it's you who have been using it.

Conversion begins at the station of surrender.

"Take up your bed and walk" (John 5:8 AKJV) describes the level of responsibility that each sinner must bear if there is to be spiritual victories in their personal lives. The word *sanctification* is summarily used to describe that walk with God. When the sinner accepts responsibilities for their imperfections and surrenders that faulty package to God through Jesus Christ, an exchange takes place that will eternally benefit the sinner.

Jesus Christ gives to us the guarantee that we will receive His forgiveness as we make bare to him our strengths and weaknesses. He does not require us to be celebrants of triumph or require that we expunge ourselves of shameful desires, vices, or feelings of guilt before approaching Him. On the contrary, Jesus Christ is requesting that those indescribable desires, godly and ungodly, be presented to Him, and He will provide the wisdom for how to handle them. The sinner who comes boldly confessing sins and heartily desirous of change will at the moment of surrender receive support to continue the journey. There is no perfection at the poolside:

> In these lay a great multitude of impotent folk, of blind, halt, withered, waiting for the moving of the water. (John 5:3 AKJV)

> Crowds of sick people—blind, lame, or paralyzed—lay on the porches. (John 5:3 NLT)

> Crowds of sick folks—lame, blind, or with paralyzed limbs—lay on the platforms (waiting for a certain movement of the water. (John 5:3 TLB)

> In these lay many invalids—blind, lame, and paralyzed. (John 5:3 NRSV)

"Take up your bed and walk" (John 5:8 AKJV) is a call for a renewed life. The Gospel of John 5:1–15 (AKJV) narrated an account of a man who was physically incapacitated and socially bound. He was defined by his illness, and to this day, he is identified as "the man by the pool of Bethesda." It is significant to note that the impotent man was located at the pool because of his sickness. He had had that sickness for thirty-eight years. From a psycho-social standpoint, he had been ill for the majority of his productive life. If he became ill at five years old, then he would have been forty-three years old when Jesus found him. If he were ten years old when he became ill, then he would have been forty-eight years when Jesus emancipated him. If the sickness attacked his body at fifteen years old, then he would have been fifty-three years when Jesus liberated him.

Dear reader, by all accounts of compassionate assessment, that man was significantly disadvantaged by the illness for an appreciable part of his life, regrettably so. His expectations of life were different from the average neighbor. He was a victim of sin. He was the victim of location. He was a victim of circumstance. He was a victim of society. But in all of this, there was hope in his heart, and his spirit was buoyed. His cup of expectation was empty, but he lived each day expecting it to be filled.

Someone may have brought you to the pool, but you will walk yourself out from the poolside.

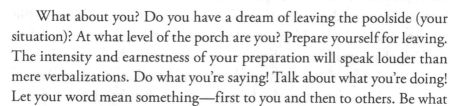

What about you? Do you have a dream of leaving the poolside (your situation)? At what level of the porch are you? Prepare yourself for leaving. The intensity and earnestness of your preparation will speak louder than mere verbalizations. Do what you're saying! Talk about what you're doing! Let your word mean something—first to you and then to others. Be what you say you want. Do what you say you want. Be it!

The day arrived when Jesus looked upon that man. What stands out is not how Jesus found him; it is the way Jesus left him. He was physically limited but spiritually charged. He was ready for his healing. What establishes this remembrance of him was not the thirty-eight years of incapacitation or the Bethesda poolside hospitalization; it was the expression of his faith and hunger for transformation. What crowns him is not his valiant fight to get to the pool but his dogged perseverance to be made well. On the day that Jesus looked upon him, that man was ready for the opportunity. He had been told that he needed to get to the pool to be made well, but his heart was expecting a transformation that was bigger than the pool. He was ready for the opportunity and did not waste it. The command of Jesus to "take up your bed and walk" (John 5:8 AKJV) was exactly what he was waiting for.

In all cases, your situation should not be your destination.

Jesus asked him to do what he had not been able to do before now. He was asked to take care of his own business. He was told that he should not depend on someone to get him to the water but to access the water by himself. He wanted to get to the pool of stirred water, but the Water of life came to him and stirred him up. He wanted help to get to the pool, but the Help that came from up above assisted him beyond his biggest dreams. Jesus canceled his dependency syndrome and gave him authority for his tomorrow. He no longer needed help to walk. Rather than being assisted, he now had the capacity to be of assistance to someone else.

Too often, where we are in life is because we are too dependent on those around us who are themselves incapacitated. We get too comfortable asking the wrong group of people for help. We blame them for not reaching out to us, thinking that they are treating us badly when they really have no way of helping us get out of the pit where we are located. We need help from outside that territory. We need power from outside of us. We need to be willing to do what we have not previously done if we are to get what we have not gotten before. It is going to require greater effort, greater faith, stronger determination, and deeper commitment.

Jesus asked him to make the effort to pick up his bed. In other words, the man who needed to be healed had to identify with his bed, symbolic of his past time and comfort, if he had to benefit from the words of his Emancipator. He was not to disavow his past. He may not have been proud of it, but it was his story. It was his experience. It was his history. Nothing could disconnect him from it but a revolutionized future. Jesus did not ask him to walk away from the bed and walk into a new direction. No! This is a troubling part of the narration.

In many settings, not excluding the church, the newly converted are given a detailed list of things to come with in worship, not including anything that reminds them of their past. The embellishment of the past should never be the attitude of the one journeying with God. However, when we remain conscious of our origins and the colossal cost of getting us out of our dismal experiences, we are gracious to others who are yet to pick up their beds and walk. We pray to God for the capacity, that allows us to be touched by the infirmities of others. The absence of the capacity to reach out to hurting people is a cogent reflection of how forgetful we have become of their past.

Always remember that everyone has a past and that that past has some parts, if not all, that many would wish on any given moment to forget. So what if you failed the first time and the second time and the third time and the fourth time and the fifth time at getting healed? So what if you fell flat on your face every time you tried to get to the pool? Do it again! Continue from where you fell. Start again—and don't give up! So what if you tried many times to get to the pool, and all of those times, someone you deemed undeserving got there before you did? What if you were a negligent parent and did not pay attention to the finer virtues of parenting? Yes, you did a terrible job, but you're still alive. Do all you can, seek the forgiveness of your children, and reconnect with them. So what if you're on your second marriage and have regrets over how you handled issues in your first marriage? Seek forgiveness with yourself and pursue forgiveness with your ex-spouse if it is still possible. What you must not do is spend a lifetime at the pool because you had some failures. Own your past, firmly use it to liberate yourself, and set on fire your passion for wholesome living.

Wouldn't it have been better to leave the bed behind to disassociate himself with impotence, poolside hospitalization, failures, and friendships?

Yes, you may argue. Of course, yes! This may have been your preference. Jesus asked him to identify with his past as he walked away from the poolside. Jesus was asking him to remember where "you were when I met you."

Remember your failures when I came to you. Remember your incapacities when I approached you and the explanations you gave me for being where you were at that time in your life. Remember to identify with those you left behind. Remember the commonalities and your history. Pick up that bed and remember you need healing and did not just arrive where you now are. You went through the waiting process, the anxious period, the moments of anguish, and the doubtful days.

Remember when I asked you if you wanted to get well? All you spilled out were excuses that you thought were reasonable. "Take up your bed and walk" (John 5:8 AKJV) away from your past, but never believe that you're better than everybody else. Now go and commit to a different future.

The joy of our souls resurrects from the moment we recognize the need to surrender to the higher calling: the salvation of our souls and the salvation of humankind. The higher calling is summed up in the two commandments as spoken by Jesus: love to God and love to all humankind.

We often get too comfortable asking the wrong people for help.

The higher calling of each heart is the decision to be selfless, to be spiritually connected to the Creative Source of all good, to the Creator of all things, to the Restorer of all good, to the Champion of all tests, to the Wisdom of the ages, to the Provider of all needs, to the Protector from all evil, to the Rock of the ages, to the Shelter in all storms, to the Destroyer of all invasions, to the Hope of the ages, to the Solution of all conflicts, to the Redeemer of humankind, to the sin-pardoning Savior, to the Anchor of all instabilities, to the Forgiver of all trespasses, to the Compass of all destinations, to the Rescuer in all emergencies, and to the Best Friend of all the destitute. When the will is surrendered to God, greatness is defined by service that is in tune with God's plan for our lives. The man at the pool was limited by circumstances; he was clearly out of sync with God's plan for his life. How do I know? The answer is in the question that Jesus asked; "Do you want to be made well?" That led to Jesus saying, "Take up your bed and walk"(John 5:8 AKJV).

"Take up your bed and walk" (John 5:8 AKJV) is a prelude to a phenomenal experience. The command to pick up the bed and walk was a call to relocate from the poolside. His time for that location was over. He was about to enter a new season in his life. That season would not be overshadowed with the poolside experience but with the phenomenal expression of faith. The poolside was not his destination. For a period, he was at the poolside, but for the next season, those who knew him there would remember him as "having been there but left fully restored, without getting into the pool."

Too often, persons who experience hardship, failure, and disappointments settle for less out of lack of a desire to relocate their hurts or their successes. God always has greatness in mind for His creation. Poolside, for many, may be relationship misfortune, divorce, or separation. For others, it may be bankruptcy or other dismal financial woes. For others, it may be confrontations with the law, including arrests and criminal charges. None of those experiences should be given the key to your future.

If you believe that God has your life in His hands and that He favors you, hardships will not be allowed to define you or design your future. Relocate despair, hurt, and disappointment to the back of the line and advance victories to the front of the line. Banish doubt, confusion, and anxieties to the back of the line. Relocate all unpleasantries to history and commit yourself to a phenomenal experience with God.

"Take up your bed and walk" (John 5:8 AKJV) is a blank canvas with your name etched on all four corners. God has handed to you a paintbrush with His commitment to help you paint. Know and understand that the one who acknowledges the need for God's presence in their life is inadvertently admitting their limitations and the need to renounce self-pride. With the opportunities given through Jesus Christ, there is no limit to achievements of any kind for those who stand on the Word of God.

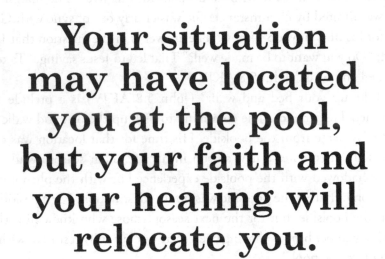

Your situation may have located you at the pool, but your faith and your healing will relocate you.

ASSESSMENT QUESTIONS

What is my current location on my life's journey?

_____

_____

How long have I been in that location?

_____

_____

Am I settling there? What are the indicators that I'm not settling?

_____

_____

Do I have intentions to relocate?

_____

_____

If yes, what am I doing about my intention to relocate from this pool of undesirable circumstances?

_____

_____

How earnest are my efforts to relocate?

_____

_____

What acquaintances, associations, and friendships have I developed over the years? How profitable have they been to my social and spiritual health?

_____

_____

How willing am I to accept the impotency that resulted in my current location?

_____

_____

Your challenge is not unique to you, but your approach to it will characterize you.
Quit stopping yourself!

CHAPTER 9

The Fear of Potential

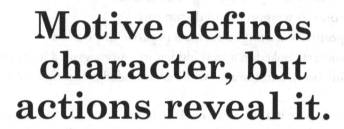

Motive defines character, but actions reveal it.

Potential is often intellectualized. It is the closest asset possessed by humankind, that can be compared to the dynamic creative power of God. It is our innate capacity to expand beyond what we now see, feel, hear, taste, and touch. It is one of God's gifts to humankind.

Go ahead and embrace that existential reality! I need you to! While you're at it, dismiss the lie that "some of us have potential and others are dumb." No! No! No! Everyone has potential. Everyone has the potential of becoming more than they presently are, acquiring more than we presently have, being professionally elevated from our current positions, being in a better relationship as father, mother, child, wife, husband, girlfriend, boyfriend. It is available to all of us.

Adopting this position requires the rejection of fearful dispositions and an acceptance of courage, discipline, and determination for all goal setters, achievers, and leaders. The sooner we accept this, the faster we will be on our journey to spiritual maturity, the quintessential level of success. When we accept that the potential in us was given to us by God, we will be better able to appreciate the urgency of investing in ourselves and the world around us.

Potential is:

- opportunity waiting to be revealed
- capital wealth hidden in an old chest, somewhere in the basement of a retired professional or the attic of an abandoned house.
- magic waiting to mesmerize the curious juices of anxious spectators
- an unused engine waiting to be tested
- comfort wrapped up in discomfort
- positivity waiting to escape a negative disposition
- success choked in a seed hidden in a stonewashed jeans pocket
- life bottled inside a jar while surrounded by drought and famine

There is potential in all of us. It is inherent in all of God's creation. Even if you choose to not believe in creation, you will have to conclude that there is in humanity greater resilience than is often acknowledged. That resilience is a by-product of the potential that waits to be discovered in you.

Have you ever wondered what it would be like to pretend God knows what you're thinking, what you like, what you've done, what you've said, what you feel, what you want, or even what you think about Him? Maybe you won't allow your mind to wander into those areas because you're afraid He will withdraw your potential for greatness. Maybe, it is because it's being used inappropriately. This is a neurotic thought.

Present your fear of God to God Himself. It is better to inform God of the fear you have of Him than to profess spiritual boldness—only to be walking on eggshells in your relationship with Him. It is better to be expressively disagreeable with God about your fear of Him than to be agreeable in words, revengeful in demeanor, and oppositional in your actions with Him. There is no way of hiding who you are from the all-seeing eyes of God.

Undeniably, who we are reflects our consciousness or lack of consciousness of God. Our acceptance of His reality motivates our appreciation for His interests in the development of our potential. No one, therefore, should have any fear of the vast interests that God has in our lives.

People ask, "Why are Christians fearful of developing their potential?"

I immediately respond, "Fear!" I also reference Matthew 19:24 (NLT): "I'll say it again—it is easier for a camel to go through the eye of a needle than for a rich person to enter the kingdom of God!" The answer is locked up in that text.

Many persons who consider their potential and what they believe they are capable of achieving or what they wish to achieve in life express fear of committing to Christianity. A plethora of reasons exists for that. At the top of the long list is the fear that submitting to the beliefs of Christianity, essentially the principles of Jesus Christ, would mean surrendering their potential to a system of beliefs that favors poverty as the expression of servanthood, humility, and nobleness.

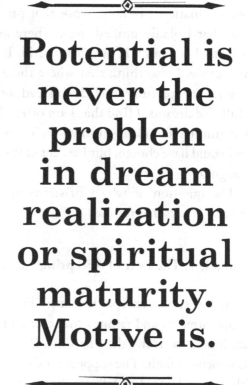

Potential is never the problem in dream realization or spiritual maturity. Motive is.

Although I don't subscribe to all the reasons advanced by the dissenters of Christianity, I can certainly agree that the fear of developing innate potential is a fear I have personally experienced. Those fears were directly linked to the scripture text quoted above: "It is easier for a camel to go through the eye of a needle than a rich man person to enter the kingdom of God" (Matthew 19:24 NLT). This, for me, is not very troubling since I have knowledge of the scriptures and the multiple pronouncements that speak to the development of human potential. However, it cannot be overlooked that the text expresses the enormous challenge that a rich person would face to make it into the kingdom of God.

So many people fear getting more than they have, reaching beyond what they have allowed themselves to believe they can reach, settling for less than their potential, and disappointing themselves and the world around them. Rich in the text includes financial wealth and does not exclude fame, academic prowess, or political power.

As I write, I remain conscious of the several opportunities outside of denominational pastoral work that presented themselves to me and those that I gladly mulled over. There are many ways of presenting the Gospel of Jesus Christ to the world. It really doesn't have to be the way I chose. I also think that where there is commitment, enthusiasm is more purposefully fueled. Instead of blaming God for present unfulfilled dreams, I find that I am often the problem with unimproved opportunities and delays in my life. There are many other career paths that I could have chosen, but I accepted this one and now have to journey through it.

The question of why Christians are fearful of developing their potential is personal for me.

Rationale 1: The Fear of Accepting Responsibility

We more easily accept responsibility for achievements, than for disappointments and failures that come with the process to achieve. We want it done correctly the first time. If it does not happen that way, then it is someone's fault. The support for this rationale is our desire to identify with success instead of failure. Parents toot the academic horns of their exceptional children and hope that the same question is not asked about other children in their families. Professionals gravitate toward other professionals whose résumés appeal to their goals and academic fantasies. The psychological motivation is to identify with the attractive, the noble, the trustworthy, and the crème de la crème and patronize the struggling. That way, the ego is satisfied temporarily, and feelings of disappointment are lowered.

The issue with this irresponsible rationale is that someone else is always the problem. It is not me. Ownership of disappointments, mishaps, and failures are easily imposed on someone else to satisfy our defensive desire to be accepted by our desirable group. When we blame someone else, the responsibility of undesirable results shifts from us to a place of less resistance and less consequence. Relentless as the thought may be, time quickly refutes it with glaring disappointment.

Shifting ownership of responsibilities provides a platform for comparisons. I am not like them. I know I'm better than them. Those of the Judeo-Christian tradition will understand the sentiments when we say, "I am not like the scribes and Pharisees." I am not a hypocrite. I know how responsible I am. Do you really know—or are you assuming that you are to deflect how much you're not? It's really important that you know if you are a responsible individual.

> # The issue with being irresponsible is that someone else is always the problem. Never me!

In my walk with God, I have discovered that there are things I would not want to tell Him and that I'd prefer He does not know. My preference is that God only discovers the things that make me comfortable. I would not want him to find out where I lack sincerity or where I am a disciple at heart. I know I'm not alone with this truth. It's like Christians with marked Bibles, but the only places marked are the promises and not the rebukes, confrontations, and stern condemnations spoken directly by God or through His mouthpieces.

If I am to be a responsible Christian, I need to observe the stern rebukes given to the religious leaders of the day as well: "But woe to you, scribes and Pharisees, hypocrites" (Matthew 23:13–39 NKJV). It is necessary that I do because I am convinced that God still speaks today as He did then. God still disciplines today as He did then. God still restores today as He did then. Further, if I accept that the scriptures are inspired, then I am obligated to believe God is holding me accountable for the totality of my potential—not excluding my spiritual development.

Rationale 2: The Fear of Others' Perception

We all are impacted in the short term or long term by the impression others have of us, especially when the unfavorable conclusion was drawn by those we revere or those who we wish would have a positive perception of us. People's perceptions of what, where, why, and how things can be done are considered constructive criticism if they have a history of success. Feedback from negative individuals is generally seen as intrusively unwelcome. We cannot run away from the threat of negative perception. Though unwanted and sometimes unjustified, perception impacts the successful as well as the unsuccessful person.

Why do the perceptions of others matter so much? It is because our success is also motivated by the fear of failure more than the acceptance of discomfort on our journey. It matters because we inadvertently appeal to the critique of others when we demonstrate our potential. Potential is raw material. Raw material does not translate into anything usable without going through a process. Everything humans possess today went through a developmental process. It is so for the medical doctor who exits the double doors of the emergency room from a successful surgery and the pastor who exits the pulpit having delivered the Word of God to His people. Perception matters, but no one should be preoccupied with it. Perception is as seasonal as spring allergies. Unless you wish to hand over your potential to someone else, I strongly encourage you to lower your emphasis on perception and focus on the energies that are waiting to unleash your potential. That's a commitment that will benefit you and your legacy.

The perceptions of others can impact relationships of all sorts. Husbands fear the repercussions of divorce and do not terminate the marriage, which they claim makes them woefully unhappy. Many couples fear the devastating effects of separation and divorce on their children; consequently, they forfeit other relationships in favor of providing their children home stability, and they proceed with the divorce when their last child gets into college.

Many parents will increase their debts for fear that if they don't, their children will not have a chance of attending college. Many children return home after college because they fear losing their inheritances if they stay away from their parents. Many employers want to terminate staff but seek a legal loophole to avoid paying gratuities or pensions. Many employees seek ways to file lawsuits against employers who have been malicious in their treatment of staff. Fear of the perceptions of others would keep all of those relationships together, miserably so.

Rationale 3: Accountability

Human beings have difficulty accepting the need to be held accountable for their actions. The fear of knowing that accountability brings the assessment of potential, scares the living daylight out of many. Instead of focusing on the development of raw potential, appreciable time is consumed marinating history, fears, weaknesses, mistakes, inferiorities, and potential failure. Consequently, less gain is achieved, and disappointment sets in.

Each of us will have to give an account of the time, talents, opportunities, and gifts that we are afforded in this life. Stewardship demands accountability. For accountability to be sincere, service must also be sincere. The absence of sincerity discolors the relationship and produces falsehoods mirrored as faithful support for the relationship. Fear undergirds such works. Jacob describes the Lord as the "fear of Isaac" his father (Genesis 31:42; cf. v. 53 AKJV), suggesting that Isaac had such reverential submission to the Lord that the Lord had to him, which was the embodiment of fear.

Rationale 4 : Motive

The reasons for doing what we do defines who we are. Motive, when unguided, has the potential to create chaos. Even more importantly, motive can mismanage the passion, resilience, and commitment that are needed to develop potential. Motive is the heart of every action and the nucleus of life or death. It must be understood that actions only reveal the character that sets motive in motion. Words, unsubstantiated by sincerity or flowing out of commitment, mean nothing. Tough statement?

Jesus emphasized that principle:

> Not every one that saith unto me, Lord, Lord, shall enter into the kingdom of heaven; but he that doeth the will of my Father which is in heaven. Many will say to me in that day, Lord, Lord, have we not prophesied in thy name? and in thy name have cast out devils? and in thy name done many wonderful works? And then will I profess unto them, I never knew you: depart from me, ye that work iniquity. (Matthew 7:21–23 AKJV)

I read a story a few decades ago about a businessman who made a significant investment in his workers shortly before he left on an extended trip. Indiscriminatingly, he invested in the workers according to the abilities assessed of them. Of the three workers chosen for the investment, one was given five thousand dollars, another two thousand, and a third one thousand. Off he went on his trip. The worker with the largest investment went to work and doubled his employer's investment. The second worker did the same. The worker with one thousand dollars, without hesitation, dug a hole and carefully buried his investment.

The trip ended, and the businessman returned home. The three workers were summoned to account for their operations. The one given five thousand dollars reported 100 percent investment, doubled his investment, presenting twice the amount delegated to him. The investor said, "Good job! You did well. You met my expectations. You believed and demonstrated your conviction that there's more you can do with whatever little that is given to you. You understood your worth. Now we are partners."

The worker with the two thousand stood up and presented his report. Like his colleague, he also had doubled the investor's investment. His employer said, "Good job! You did well. You met my expectations. I knew I could have counted on you risking it all so you could gain more. You understood your worth. You invested in yourself. Now we are partners."

Last and unexpectedly least, the employee who was given one thousand dollars said, "Sir, I know you have high standards, hate careless ways, demand the best, and make no allowances for error. I played it safe. I took no unnecessary risk. I was afraid I might disappoint you. I did not want to risk losing anything you gave me, so I found a good hiding place and secured your money. Here it is, safe and sound, down to the last cent. I really hope you understand my decision and appreciate my risk-management plan."

The businessman took umbrage to the attitude and response of the employee. More vilifying than the worker's attitude and response was the perception of the businessman. Wrath gripped the atmosphere as the employee was reprimanded for being shortsighted, overly careful, fearful, insolent, unambiguously selfish, and self-serving. The businessman said, "If you knew I was unreasonable, demanding, and favored excellence, that I was after the best, why did you do less than the least? The least you could have done was invest the sum with the bankers. At least you would have gotten a little interest. But no, you dug a hole and buried your investment. You lost an opportunity to be a partner with me."

The story ended with the instruction given to reward the greatest risk taker with the initial capital of the least risk taker (though he had the least risk) and to remove him from the company of risk takers. (Matthew 25:14–30 AKJV)

It is significant to note the attitude of the businessman toward his three workers. Recognize the investor gave to his workers according to his knowledge of and assignment for them and not their expectation of him or according to what the servants may have thought of themselves. The initiative was his. The authority was his. They were in his jurisdiction and dependent on him for daily sustenance. The owner was the one who had done the assessment. He initiated the call. He gave of his resources for the development of their potential.

The circumstances surrounding the distribution of the investment seed is another principle that is often missed in that parable. Although the

Bible does not indicate any differences in the time when the servants were given their talents (investment potential), there is sufficient information to support the image of the servants receiving their investments at the same time. First the five, then the two, and thirdly the one talent. If they were in the same location at the disbursement, with sight and knowledge of what each received, the atmosphere could have brought to bear hidden issues of jealousy and perceptions of unfairness that secretly occupied the hearts of the servants.

The one with the five talents was further rewarded at the end of the allotted investment period. Recognize there was no difference in the amount of time the servants had to make the investments. They all had their opportunities during the absence of the businessman, which was the same period of time. He had the same expectations of them. One may argue that there was a disparity in the quantities allotted. Indeed, there was. Nevertheless, the potential of a great reward did not depend in the quantity but in the attitude toward the potential gifted him. Our uniqueness should not be regarded as insignificance. Uniqueness is creativity spoken in a language that visionary minds can capture. Less should not be translated to mean insignificant. Rather, less in the lens of the visionary is opportunity for more. If we can develop the attitude of gratefulness when less is what we possess, then our creative energies will only serve to motivate us to invest what is in our hands. Every situation is always self-defined. It needs no further definition. Instead of investing limited resources in the promotion of self-hate, seek to understand existing limitations as unique opportunities for expansion.

Attention must be given to the decision of the investor to increase the resources of the one who already had the greatest investment returns. The position raises the question of economic disparity and the creation or support of a class system. Instead of rewarding the "overly careful," "non-risk-taking" attitude of his servant, the master rewarded the conviction of the one who had more talents yet risked losing it all so that he may give the best account of himself when his investor returns. The principle here is that the one who desires to achieve much must be willing to risk much. There is comfort in safety and discomfort in taking risks. However, it is in discomfort that we experience the need for better, for more, for greater, for excellence, and for best.

Three attitudes stood out to me in that parable. Firstly, all three employees demonstrated the conviction that the investor would have returned and needed to be given an investment report. Secondly, two of the employees approached the opportunity with a constructive attitude. They saw potential development, freedom from marginalization, and opportunity for partnership with their employer. Though void of their employer's unspoken motive, they understood the timeliness and graciousness of opportunity knocking at their door. The third attitude really concerned me. It was the cherished negative perception of the investor (master as per parable, businessman as per attitude, redeemer as per consolation), which led to the demise of the employee. He failed at self-improvement, at territorial expansion, and potential development because disconcerting view of the investor resided in him. Multiple lessons can be learned from that disposition. I will highlight the obvious one: Negativity only keeps subtracting from productivity.

Did you know that many Christians fear the demands of risking to win? Have you not heard that the cost of production has kept many from achieving? Have you not read that it is not the absence of potential that has significantly paralyzed the future of many wannabe achievers? They are aware of their potential but lack the courage to take it from the stagnation phase to the production phase. Consequently, they misrepresent God's favor in their lives. They blame God for not having blessed them with sufficient opportunities for expansion and for increase. They argue against blessing in disparity and blessing by selection.

How can some be blessed by God and others are not? According to the apostle Paul, the one aiming to win must self-examine, become self-aware, self-accept, commit, and dedicate every ounce of potential to achieving the coveted prize.

> Not as though I had already attained, either were already perfect: but I follow after, if that I may apprehend that for which also I am apprehended of Christ Jesus. Brethren, I count not myself to have apprehended: but this one thing I do, forgetting those things which are behind, and reaching forth unto those things which are before, I press

toward the mark for the prize of the high calling of God
in Christ Jesus. (Philippians 3:12–14 AKJV)

I've witnessed many students with phenomenal potential, but they have consented with circumstances to settle for average. Some will cling to their financial woes as a reason to not pursue their academic dreams or start that business that will provide a way out of their present situation. Others justify their inactivity to produce by using their history as an escape.

Refuse to settle! Keep winning task after task. Success will represent the struggles of your years and the capacity of your heart to endure all things. With every win, you are building the structure that represents determination, dedication, resilience, and obedience built under hardship, in humility, and for all eternity. Keep winning. The winner is one who has not learned that it's impossible to win. The high achiever is a loser transformed by heart dedication, resolute attitude, and belief in the power of God. You, certainly, are not the only one of whom the universe will demand commitment, but you will surely be the one who will be denied entrance to the company of achievers because of your fear of developing your potential. What will it be for you?

The winner is one who has not learned that it's impossible to win.

The Christian is not to be ashamed of winning, being successful, or being a high achiever. Such thinking is anathema to the benefit of a faithful relationship with God. God's expectation is that He will be the priority in the lives of His creation. The requisite instruction on how to win is to seek God first. Give him first place. Give him first allegiance. Give him first consideration. Let him be the first thought. He has knowledge of the terrain that you will journey. The complete valley is before him, and the strategies of the adversary are identifiable by him. Courage is required to win. Blaming circumstances is surely not one of them.

> No temptation has overtaken you except what is common to mankind. And God is faithful; he will not let you be tempted beyond what you can bear. But when you are tempted, he will also provide a way out so that you can endure it. (1 Corinthians 10:13 NIV)

> No weapon that is formed against thee shall prosper; and every tongue that shall rise against thee in judgment thou shalt condemn. This is the heritage of the servants of the Lord, and their righteousness is of me, saith the Lord. (Isaiah 54:17 AKJV)

Fear is responsible for the reluctance of many to bear witness of their convictions. This was evident in the ministry of Jesus:

> Yet for fear of the Jews no one spoke openly of him. (John 7:13 NIV)

> Later, Joseph of Arimathea asked Pilate for the body of Jesus. Now Joseph was a disciple of Jesus, but secretly because he feared the Jewish leaders. With Pilate's permission, he came and took the body away. (John 19:38 NIV)

Fear of persecution kept Christians in hiding.

> On the evening of that first day of the week, when the disciples were together, with the doors locked for fear of

the Jewish leaders, Jesus came and stood among them and said, "Peace be with you!" (John 20:19 NIV)

Here is the captivating point. Potential is the bridge from not knowing your worth to realizing your worth. Deciding to develop your potential, therefore, is an act of covenantal service. It is your commitment to your future. If your future will truly reflect your commitment, you must be prepared to invest your all into it. Nothing less than that amount. All! Not 80 percent, but 100 percent! If the investment does not deserve your all, then it should be classified as a nonessential for your journey.

Potential indicates capacity, but only process brings out reality. The final product reflects your understanding of your worth. No one can value the significance of your product better than you. Why? You know the cost of production. You know the pride, the fear, the anxieties, and the discomfort you went through to produce what you now have. No one is aware of the tensions, the disagreements, the highs, and the lows that preceded the product that they now hold. But you do. That's why you need to be able to answer the questions about your worth.

"How much am I worth?"

"What motivated the investment in me?"

"How will I be able to generate support for future investment in me?"

"What does it take to keep me valuable to my investor?"

The challenges in the story are also crucial to personal, relational, and organizational development. If you invest in a relationship, it is worth considering the cost just as you would if you were to invest in a multimillion-dollar corporation. Every decision matters. Every decision may not require the same level of preparation and execution, but they all carry the potential for catastrophic disappointments, feelings of rejection and regret, or celebration, satisfaction, and future motivations.

Fear of not being justly compensated will motivate you to undermine your potential. This was the crux of the employee's phobia. He said, "I cannot measure up to the standards of my employer. I know I have the raw material to grow, expand, educate myself, and invest in my family and my marriage, but I don't have the evidence that there will be reciprocity. Consequently, I will not risk any development because I just don't know."

Here is a vital takeaway from that example: The one who has little and does nothing with it does not deserve to receive more. This principle is fundamentally attached to the rhythm for unprecedented success. Success comes with an acknowledged cost. However, with the acknowledgment comes the determination to risk it all to gain inconceivably or cherish potential and lose miserably.

The fear of failing will, more than likely, materialize in colossal failure. The potential for failure cannot be obliterated in anything where human participation is a necessity. This is especially so in emotional investments such as marriage. No one builds a house before counting the cost. You and I know that, but knowing the cost does not absolve anyone from putting in the effort required to obtain the object of their dream. Count the cost and put in what it takes to get it.

The one who has little and does nothing with it does not deserve to receive more. The fear of giving your all to a person or entity that does not appreciate your gifts will demotivate you. Every human being appreciates affirmation. Some more than others, but

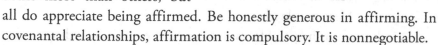

> **The one who has little and does nothing with it does not deserve to receive more.**

all do appreciate being affirmed. Be honestly generous in affirming. In covenantal relationships, affirmation is compulsory. It is nonnegotiable.

The motivation to affirm may be met with resistance at first. Don't dismiss that. Existing variables may contribute to resistance. Resistance can influence demotivation, and demotivation can lead to indifference. A variable I will recommend that all consider is the perception of the one who made the large investment in us. That judgment may be driving our demotivation and our relationship with the investor. Our children invest in us as we do in them. Our spouse is an investor in us as we are in them. Our church is an investor in us as we are in her. Our school is an investor in us as we are in it. Our society is an investor in us as we are in it. The list here is inexhaustible. On a very personal note, if you have made the recognition that your gifts are not appreciated, it is time to make the much-neglected investment in your future. It is not too early to begin today.

Fear of inadequacy and rejection will escalate if you casually manage the raw material needed to establish your legacy. Make no mistake about this. Failure to justifiably manage your resources will only increase your fear of inadequacy and rejection. Why fear inadequacy? Because you will sooner or later conclude you don't have what it takes to satisfy the covenant or provide expected services within the covenant. Why rejection? Because failure to meet standards according to what you believe is expected of you will extract from you the interpretation that your investor is displeased with your actions and will reject you.

Fear of inadequacy will increase if you esteem the gifts of others higher than your own. Here is something to remember. Everyone has potential. Further, everyone you will meet has the potential to do more than they have always been doing. That principle when applied to human interaction will encourage you to see value in everything and in everyone. Rightly understood, you will learn to appreciate differences in talents, gifts, skills, and interests and how all of this contributes to personal achievements.

Although it is commonplace to believe that someone socialized with success will desire success, it has also been evidenced that everyone who desires success, develops a realistic plan for success, works the plan successfully, makes realistic adjustments to facilitate the plan, and seeks first the kingdom of God and His righteousness will get closer and closer to amazing success than those who simply wished and never invested their raw resources. Hear me clearly!

As indicated in the parable, raw resources are given according to the assessment results. You are gifted with raw resources. Take time to appreciate that gift. Develop and execute your "how-to-win" plan. Henry Wadsworth Longfellow said, "The heights by great men reached and kept, were not attained by sudden flight, but they while their companions slept, were toiling upward through the night." I urge you, therefore, not to place greater value on anyone's resources than yours. I still believe that biblical principle taught in Sabbath school that teaches "little becomes much when we place it in the Master's hands."

Fear of losing your investment should motivate you to expend yourself in expanding its capacity to give you more. Don't settle for maintenance. You were delegated with your resources because your Master knows your potential. You have what it takes. You won't be sincerely able to say, "I gave it my all," if you didn't. It would be self-defeating to do so.

The principle of commitment to your potential is qualified by the quality of service you render. Covenantal service without fear is embedded in the life of John the apostle. Riveted to his calling, John survived vicious attacks from political and religious leaders of his day. John survived it all because God had not finished with him yet. God was preparing him for isolation on Patmos.

The revelation of the Lord Jesus Christ was still to come through him. It was in a cave on the isle of Patmos, and John was in the spirit on the Lord's Day when he received the timely word

It's impossible to feel justified to lay down your tools when there is still time to invest in yourself and in others.

from God. That timely word gave us the book of Revelation, the book that drives the apocalyptic voice of the church today.

John penned the events that surround the return of Jesus, centuries after Daniel received similar visions from God. John wrote of Jesus's Second Coming and inspired the Christian church to anticipate His glorious return. Two years after John's exile on Patmos, Emperor Domitian died, and John's exilic experience ended with his return to the church in Ephesus. The youngest of Jesus's disciples lived with resilience to be the oldest, dying in peace in Ephesus at the age of eighty after more than half a century of dedicated and watchful service to the church.

Covenantal service, driven by worship and not fear, motivates an unwavering resilience that is second to nothing. It's impossible to feel justified to lay down your tools when there is still time to invest in yourself and in others. A lecturer at Caribbean Union College decades ago, while lecturing to us ministerial students, said, "Young men, there is no retirement from God's service. There is only retirement from organizational work." In hindsight I should have asked, "Which is more enjoyable: God's service or organizational work? And does that epiphany precede or succeed retirement?"

Remember the power of potential. Inject integrity into a mosaic process, but remember to focus on results and not resistance. Identify in your composition the indubitable urge to refuse believing that you will denied what you have been promised never to be denied. The promise of Jesus is this: "And I will do whatever you ask in My name, so that the Father may be glorified in the Son. If you ask Me for anything in My name, I will do it" (John 14:13, 14 BSB). What phenomenal access we have to the unlimited resources of God.

I am enthralled by the largesse Jesus extended to His disciples. On account of Him, in His name, we have access to the throne room of God. No better illustration comes to mind than walking into one of those financial institutions in St. Lucia that seems to be more friendly to foreign borrowers than nationals and present a name authorizing me to withdraw a particular sum of money from his account. Even if I am raggedly dressed, the presentation of his permission grants me the authority to receive from the bank, from the regard the institution has for him, that which he has authorized. This is equivalent to him giving it to me in person. On a more spectacular plain, we are to go to the Father to receive what has been promised to us by Jesus Christ, in whom He is well pleased (Matthew 3:17 AKJV). We are to do it in his name and expect that the favor will be bestowed on us who are friends of His Son. Be fearless!

This is key to our success in walking with God. We ought to boldly accept the permission granted to us. Instead of burying your gifts in the ground of discouragement, for fear opportunities for territorial expansion may not come your way, for fear your employer will not recognize your efforts to invest in his cause, I strongly recommend that you start asking God to reveal to you, in a deliberate manner, your next steps in service to Him and society. It may be that your struggle is failure to recognize investment opportunities and that unimproved opportunities have led to a lethargic experience. Perhaps you have concluded your service without being acknowledged or appreciated and therefore have questioned your own usefulness in your vocation. Get busy! Get asking! God is listening!

Leave behind a legacy of covenantal service. Paint on the walls of forever, the inarguable inscription: "I came. I served faithfully and transitioned heartily." Render love to the loveless. Give comfort to the lonely. Establish hope in the hopeless. Transmit joy to the joyless. Give strength to the weak. Feed the hungry. Clothe the naked! Bring cheer to the sorrowed. Liberate those in captivity. Advocate for the voiceless. But whatever you do, know that the fear of the Lord is an inducement to obedience and service and that to rightfully fear God is to execute His will. Serve the Lord as evidence of proper recognition of His sovereignty. Do not fear the challenge. Instead, let your report be that you have effectively transformed every available opportunity, that you quantifiably increase your master's trust, and that you're satisfied you exuded hope every step of your journey.

Seek earnestly to understand what is in your hands. Purpose to use what is in your hands. Invest in you and others. Serve others as you would serve you.

ASSESSMENT QUESTIONS

What potential lies in my hands? What gifts do I possess?

_____

_____

If I have discovered my gifts, how willing and committed am I to utilizing it/them to the blessing of myself and others?

_____

_____

Do I know that my gift/gifts is/are indelibly tied to my purpose?

_____

_____

When was the last time I reassessed the progress I've made on the fulfillment of my purpose?

_____

_____

Understanding my purpose and the value of my investment, what is it going to take for me to improve myself?

_____

_____

Did my investor see more in me than I have recognized in myself? Am I shortchanging myself here by thinking less of me?

_____

_____

What is the value of what I have in me?

_____

_____

How satisfied would I be if I didn't use the gifts/talents/skills that I know I have?

_____

_____

But even if you should suffer for what is right, you are blessed: "Do not fear their threats; do not be frightened"

(1Peter 3:14 NIV).

CHAPTER 10

The Fear of Temptation

Can you remember your first temptation? At least try to do so. Was it the proverbial red apple? What about the second one or the third one? What about the fifth, sixth, seventh, or twelfth temptation?

Okay, let me stop tempting you to go so far back in time and reconnect with something you may or may not be pleased with. I'm still curious to know one thing, as well as to help clarify something in your thoughts. How did you know that experience, whatever it was, was a temptation? How did you know? If you knew it was a temptation, what about it

Temptation is real. The struggle is real. So is the power to overcome.

resonated with you? I'm certain you cannot remember your first temptation, the place where you were first tempted, and the time or the circumstances surrounding that temptation. Despite the honest amnesia, temptation was real then and will continue to be for every one of us.

I have absolutely no recollection of the time, place, circumstance, or motivation of my first temptation. I may have very well not recognized the gravity of it and may have acquiesced. But how can I be so certain if I have no knowledge of it? It is because my first temptation had to have been after the time I became knowledgeable of right and wrong. In recollection, I was always fearful of knowing what was wrong, but I had great curiosity about discovering what was right. As a matter of fact, I remember plunging myself into opportunities that emphasized and reflected worship to avoid the possibility of inadvertently encountering temptations of any sort.

What about temptation welds so much fear in the hearts of humankind? There is a qualified response in the writings of the apostle James 1:13–16 (NLT):

> And remember, when you are being tempted, do not say, "God is tempting me." God is never tempted to do wrong, and he never tempts anyone else. Temptation comes from our own desires, which entice us and drag us away. These desires give birth to sinful actions. And when sin is allowed to grow, it gives birth to death. So don't be misled, my dear brothers and sisters.

Temptation has an evil reputation and an intentionally selfish agenda. It is the cunning, approachable, nonconfrontational, angel of light, yet its overpowering, domineering nature of temptations stupefies the hearts of humankind. Temptation is connoted with feelings, misapplications, and misjudgments even when understanding and imageries of right and wrong may be evident.

The philosophical underpinning of temptation is that a person has been wired to do otherwise, but for reasons that they accept to be beneficial to them, they may decide to do differently because the contrary benefits present, for the most part, as immediately more pleasurable, sustaining or, beneficial and can possibly carry over into the future. Temptation answers to moods, fancies, anxieties, and emotions and not rational, elaborate, and logical cogitations or right and wrong. For example, I'm so excited about typing this chapter, but I'm itching to stop just to pick up my phone and chitchat with friends I've not heard from in a long while. I'm quite sure we'd have some laughter, but I'm resisting because the benefits of completing this work on schedule, in my rational estimation, far outweigh the conversations that I could have been having with persons who had decided not to return my calls or contact me in months.

In my teens, I was of the conviction that temptation always had to do with sexual sins. Seriously, I did. I was definitely impacted by my context, home, school, and church life. My mind goes to a favorite hymn sung by my church. "Yield Not to Temptation" has meaningful words and overpowering ethos. The musical arrangements so melodiously embraced the voices of the mothers and fathers of the congregation that I learned the hymn by de facto interest and fear. I was afraid that I was guilty of all sins even if I did not understand all temptations. My understanding was that I should not give in to temptations because I would be displeasing God. So, in my teens, I struggled with developing interest in the opposite sex because I understood them to be the conduit for sinfulness and a sure downward path away from God. From my understanding of temptation, it was safer to be alone with myself or maintain friendships with other males. This hymn would not leave my head:

> Yield not to temptation,
> For yielding is sin;
> Each vict'ry will help you,
> Some other to win;
> Fight valiantly onward,
> Evil passions subdue;
> Look ever to Jesus,
> He will carry you through.
>
> Refrain:
> Ask the Savior to help you,
> Comfort, strengthen and keep you;
> He is willing to aid you,
> He will carry you through.

Shun evil companions,
Bad language disdain;
God's name hold in rev'rence,
Nor take it in vain;
Be thoughtful and earnest,
Kindhearted and true;
Look ever to Jesus,
He will carry you through.

To him that o'ercometh,
God giveth a crown;
Through faith we will conquer,
Though often cast down;
He who is our Saviour,
Our strength will renew;
Look ever to Jesus,
He will carry you through.
(Horatio R. Palmer, 1868)

I also struggled with the temptation conundrum during adolescence and early adulthood. I found myself interpreting choices as sinful because I had to choose between what someone told me was right for me and what I have come to accept as more beneficial to me for my life goals. I had to learn to understand the differences between evil and good, especially because everything that I was told was good or evil accompanied the biased conviction of the one who told me. I had to understand for myself the preferences imposed on me and the appropriateness of those preferences for the virtues I was willing to uphold.

Please don't misunderstand me. I am not saying everything I was taught was wrong! I am making the point that I had to recognize that even those who taught me had preferences for some things and did not regard those as sinful, but those for which they did not have a proclivity was for the most part labelled ungodly, immoral, sinful, or too close to sinfulness to have any shade of righteousness in them.

I had to establish personal virtues and preferences. Though impacted by influential seniors, they had become mine, and I owned the philosophical positions and the satisfaction they brought to my life. Exercising most of my untapped choices led to discoveries that phenomenally empowered my life to the amazement of many and the disappointment of others.

Discovery 1

Temptation is not sin. What an exhilarating discovery! Inherent in that statement is the penultimate solution to every choice one would make from the moment of its acceptance to the last millisecond of its application. For me, it was a liberating discovery then and still is today. There is nothing significant about that discovery; you may be tempted to say. Not true!

Let me hasten to share with you that the knowledge itself dismantles all barriers to self-awareness, self-love, and development. No longer would you be afraid to discover you, thinking you are the reason why temptations exist, but that you also have knowledge it is not harmful for you to discover yourself. On the contrary, you need to be discovered. You are waiting to be discovered. You are waiting to get familiar with yourself.

Having the knowledge that temptation is not sin should motivate you to love and not beat up on yourself for what you have not understood about you. Often, the reason for beating up yourself is what someone dislikes about you but is not bad for you. Just because they dislike it does not mean it is not elevating to you or should not be used to elevate others who are different from them. That knowledge is empowering because you will learn to accept that you don't have to speed-dial temptation's headquarters and request a temptation, but the headquarters has spies commissioned to subtly influence you to remain ignorant of their presence, influence, and agenda. Indeed, knowledge is empowering and elevating.

Discovery 2

It is not sinful for you to be tempted or to recognize temptation's insistence to deliberately debilitate your walk with God. Remember, we do not have to request that temptations be sent to us. (Pay attention to this statement. It may save your life). Temptations will inevitably find us wherever we are.

Humanity is sinful, carnal, and sold under sin and its desires. The law is spiritual, but I am carnal and sold under sin (Romans 7:14 KJV).

Whether it be up there in that pulpit, up in the choir loft, in the vestry, in the confession box, on the church pews, in the monastery, in your personal space at home minding your own business, in private driving space, in the classroom, or in the quietness of the university library, temptations will find us and present their supposedly best-crafted agenda. There is no place under the aged sun where temptation is unreachable. This is humbling, yet empowering. Humbling in that it crushes self-exaltation, self-worship, and religious bigotry; empowering because the sinner is compelled to accept the personal self as spiritually degenerate, carnal, and potentially self-destructive without the saving grace of Jesus Christ. It is empowering to know that it is only through the daily active surrendering of whatever desires to God through His Son, Jesus Christ, that one is able to have awareness and overcome the temptations of the adversary. It is self-destructive to deny the bombardment of any temptation hoping that the temptation will dissipate and vanish with the denial. Such a thought would prepare the way to accept the next temptation of that same type.

Discovery 3

Temptation comes to everyone differently but through the same means. This means everyone's approach to resisting temptation may not be the same. With the Bible as my guide, I will highlight humanity's struggle to do what is pleasing to God. In Romans 7 (AKJV), the apostle Paul recognized the battle to do contrary when differently should have been done. He further noted the impatience of the self to win over from doing wrong because the heart's desire is to please God. That struggle is present in the life of all humanity.

The battle is intensified when one makes a commitment to live a life totally committed to the Word of God and discover that living the commitment remains a daily uphill battle. Spiritual frustrations can result from the usual unexpected failures, and feelings of rejection from God can become a reality. This can be particularly so when oneself is compared to a known believer who does not appear to be struggling in their walk with

God. Here's a reminder: temptation comes to everyone differently but through the same means. Our senses are the only instruments used by the adversary to interrupt our walk with God.

Hearing, smelling, tasting, seeing, and touching are crucial to a successful life on earth. Those senses have been identified as a family unit that requires synchronicity for optimum benefit to humanity. Race, ethnicity, and social, economic, political, or religious status is inconsequential. The senses drive our heart's desires, and our desires, managed or mismanaged, shape our character. The significance of this understanding is highlighted in Proverbs 4:23 (NLT): "Guard your heart above all else, for it determines the course of your life."

The heart, as a pumping station, is not the parallel here, but the mind, the seat of the conscience, the executive chair from which all decisions are made, the command center where all pieces of information are reviewed and given or denied priority, the arsenal where offensive and defensive artilleries are kept, the fortress where security is ascertained and exact, the sanctuary where solitude and inspiration wait to be embraced. Guard it! Whatever it takes to keep you safe, functional, and saved, guard it!

It cannot be overemphasized that those instruments, structurally given to us in creation for self-development, healthy living, and worship of our Creator have been targeted by the adversary of souls and have now been made the battleground for the destruction of our souls. Enough attention is not paid by many to the avenues through which the enemy of souls invades our lives.

Many regard their hearts as guarded when the sentinels are asleep at the gates. It is not with the occasional assessment of spiritual values or religious programming that the spiritual soul is fortified. It is through a consistent, determined, practical, and honest effort on the part of the one who is seeking to know God for themselves. It is not with a sudden attack that the gates are brought down to the ground but through momentary failures, unheeded opportunities, impractical assessments, and false securities that the heart remains accessible, and the soul is flooded with the destructive emissaries corrupting the senses and opportunities created for the weakening of character.

Discovery 4

It is not temptation but the self that must be managed.

I will never forget a statement I read on a T-shirt: "Lead me not into temptation for I shall find it myself."

"Oh hush," I responded. "Temptation is not compelling enough to take you where it wants you to go. You don't have to want to follow."

After taking time to analyze the plea of the one tempting others like me to read the facetious intent of the statement (to allow them to choose their own temptation and not present them with one, for if it is in their desire to find it, as they may have already desired to find it, they will find it because temptation is not difficult to find), I discovered that the statement had the capacity to be confusing and misleading. It was an SOS rescue call and a warning to those who would have otherwise been contemplating a temptation for the already vulnerable. It was a call to desist from making a tempting offer for whatever thing—to whatever place and for whatever benefit—but it was intentionally inviting at best.

Temptation needs no cheerleader. Temptation's nature is fueled by its innate agenda: convincing its target otherwise establish, even if it's temporary, a significant difference between what is understood to be the right or best preferred to the acceptance of what is wrong or otherwise destructive to the ultimate fulfillment of God's desire for a person. In truth, too much time is exerted on identifying temptations compared to character development, hence the fear of temptation. If the amount of time spent in highlighting temptations is spent in building and reinforcing the walls of the hearts, our walks with God would be significantly more committed, progressive, and spiritually fulfilling. The adversary remains concealed using the subtle element of distraction.

Temptations, when targeted at humanity, must find a responding chord. The responding chord can be the residue of a previous relationship or an experience at an impressionable time in life. That reverberating chord signals a connection between the stimulus and the response. That response is what we have been working all our lives to accept or to reject. The attraction of the temptation is what the adversary believes we will find attractive. The interpretation of the attractiveness is linked to our genetic predispositions (DNA) and the lifestyle we have lived up to that point. The lifestyle includes what we have fed our eyes, noses, mouths, hands, ears, and hearts over the years and what we have inadvertently received from our environments through various stimulations.

A Father's Wise Advice

> My children, listen when your father corrects you.
> Pay attention and learn good judgment,
> for I am giving you good guidance.
> Don't turn away from my instructions.
> For I, too, was once my father's son,
> tenderly loved as my mother's only child.
>
> My father taught me,
> "Take my words to heart.
> Follow my commands, and you will live.
> Get wisdom; develop good judgment.
> Don't forget my words or turn away from them.
> Don't turn your back on wisdom, for she will protect you.
> Love her, and she will guard you.
> Getting wisdom is the wisest thing you can do!
> And whatever else you do, develop good judgment.
> If you prize wisdom, she will make you great.
> Embrace her, and she will honor you.
> She will place a lovely wreath on your head;
> she will present you with a beautiful crown."
>
> My child, listen to me and do as I say,
> and you will have a long, good life.
> I will teach you wisdom's ways
> and lead you in straight paths.
> When you walk, you won't be held back;
> when you run, you won't stumble.
> Take hold of my instructions; don't let them go.
> Guard them, for they are the key to life.

Don't do as the wicked do,
and don't follow the path of evildoers.
Don't even think about it; don't go that way.
Turn away and keep moving.
For evil people can't sleep until they've done their evil
deed for the day.
They can't rest until they've caused someone to stumble.
They eat the food of wickedness
and drink the wine of violence!

The way of the righteous is like the first gleam of dawn,
which shines ever brighter until the full light of day.
But the way of the wicked is like total darkness.
They have no idea what they are stumbling over.

My child, pay attention to what I say.
Listen carefully to my words.
Don't lose sight of them.
Let them penetrate deep into your heart,
for they bring life to those who find them,
and healing to their whole body.

Guard your heart above all else,
for it determines the course of your life.
Avoid all perverse talk;
stay away from corrupt speech.
Look straight ahead,
and fix your eyes on what lies before you.
Mark out a straight path for your feet;
stay on the safe path.
Don't get sidetracked;
keep your feet from following evil. (Proverbs 4 NLT)

This is my heart's desire, in Jesus's name, I pray. Amen. Amen. Amen!

How best we are able to decipher what is spiritually beneficial or destructive to us may not be exactly easy, but it is crucial for spiritual edification. For example, the home environment would have impacted the life of an adolescent just as society would. What produces greater impact will be different for many, but no one can escape the impact of the home and society in the development of their character.

The unmarried, sexually active individual who decides to become a Christian will not become immune to sexual temptations just as the one who is sexually inactive but actively fantasizes about that first sexual experience that seems too distant. Both individuals will need to develop character to resist the temptations that may come to them. For the previously active, it may be that I can no longer remain celibate. For the fantasizer, it may be the same. The challenge for both may be the same, but lifestyle choices will significantly influence their responses. Support from significant others and personal spiritual goals will serve to motivate a commitment to values.

Discovery 5

Fear does not obliterate temptation. This is a misnomer in the lives of some who regard fear of temptation as a safety net from its destructive intention. Others comfort themselves in the victories of previous experiences and believe they can use the same strategies, methodologies, and rescue patterns to secure another victory over a new temptation. This usually results in disappointments, and the heart is again tortured by the hands of self-deception.

In the place of fear, there should be an acknowledgement of temptation's presence as an intruder. This is the first step in understanding its impact on your walk with God. See it for what it is: an invader and an unwanted guest that is seeking to impose on you what you don't need. The entertainment of the unwanted guest will negatively influence your walk with God, your significant others, and yourself. Fear of targeting the attractiveness of the intruder should be given to the one who is "a very present help in trouble" (Psalm 46:1 AKJV).

It is possible to journey with God without the fear of temptation. It is not temptation but self-reliance that has been our downfall. Fear of yielding to temptation contributes to the denial of its presence, and where seemingly overwhelming, it floods the soul with guilt. Denial increases the overpowering nature of temptation and the unceasing bombardment on the door of the soul. The soul can stand no stronger against the towering strength of temptation than bamboo sticks can withhold the overpowering currents of a broken water dam.

It is possible to journey with God without the fear of temptation. It is not temptation, but self-reliance that has been our downfall.

Fear of temptation can influence a false sense of security in activities and relationships that seem to offer spiritual safety. That false sense of spirituality can reflect a delusion: "I am spiritually mature and therefore need no further development in necessary areas in my life." The apostle Paul cautioned the Christian church:

> Now these things happened to them as examples and were written down as warnings for us, on whom the fulfillment of the ages has come. So the one who thinks he is standing firm should be careful not to fall. No temptation has

seized you except what is common to man. And God is faithful; He will not let you be tempted beyond what you can bear. But when you are tempted, He will also provide an escape, so that you can stand up under it." (1 Corinthians 10:11–13 NIV)

Self-reliance has consistently failed all who have momentarily or protractedly tried to stand on their own in the face of temptations. Everyone has to own the individuality of their choices; sin is always personal and so are the temptations that precede it. Always remember that sinfulness as a state is not chosen because it is human nature. Therefore, immunity from temptations must never be accepted as a possibility until humanity's carnality is obliterated. The possibility of living in Jesus without the fear of temptation is a practical reality. Jesus prescribed the possibility of saving a rich man: "With man this is impossible, but not with God. For all things are possible with God" (Mark 10:27 NIV). It is possible to journey with God without the fear of temptation. Self-dependence has been the downfall of every one of us.

Discovery 6

The fear of temptation motivates some to be judgmental of others. The fear of temptation is very subtly pervasive. We have established that temptation, in order to take effect in our lives, must connect with something in us. It is bad judgment to pass judgment upon another because a temptation to which you would not respond was ground zero for someone else. Not everyone will desire to use or traffic illegal drugs, experience premarital sex, abuse alcohol, or keep an illegal firearm. However, everyone gets tempted to sin. Religious individuals seem to have almost perfected an attribute of the chameleon: to change color and sufficiently adapt to its environment. Not that the heart is transformed, but the behavior is modified to blend with the occasion. This is a spiritual challenge that highlights form without substance, presence without authenticity, and glossolalia without message.

The difficulty that many experience is the acceptance that others have sinned. Please don't accuse me of being licentious here. It may be that you, like others, need to confront the judgmental part of your character and that the proclivity to judge others is a major issue that requires your acceptance rather than denial. If you are a Christian reading this book, you're not the only one struggling with a judgmental attitude. Judgmentalism continues to survive as an acceptable sin in Christendom and is often excused with a scripture verse:

> Do not judge according to appearance, but judge with righteous judgment. (John 7:24 KJV)

> Stop judging by mere appearances, but instead judge correctly. (John 7:24 NIV)

> Look beneath the surface so you can judge correctly. (John 7:24 NLT)

So many believe that they are judging righteously when it is not so. Wrongdoing needs appropriate confrontation where it is found. However, the prescription to do so is spelled out in the Bible:

> Why do you look at the speck in your brother's eye, but fail to notice the beam in your own eye? How can you say to your brother, "Let me take the speck out of your eye" while there is still a beam in your own eye?" You hypocrite! First take the beam out of your own eye, and then you will see clearly to remove the speck from your brother's eye." (Matthew 7:3–5 KJV)

The Gospel writer penned the words of Jesus as a rebuke to dispositions of self-righteousness and vanity, character traits existent in those who fear temptations and believe admitting their vulnerabilities or sins would make them eternally lost. It is an affront in God's eyes to deny our spiritual realities and portray who we are not. Not that we become complacent or accepting of our spiritual misdemeanors or felonies. No! We accept the truth about ourselves and develop a spiritual plan for getting out of the pit where we may have fallen. This is a more courageous attitude than pretending not to have the desire to desire what you should not be desiring.

Own the desire—no matter what it is. I really do mean this for you. It is the first step in understanding how to be empathetic and sympathetic with others who have similar or different weaknesses.

The fear of owning one's sinful desires is linked to thinking, *If I accept I have that weakness or that I desire XYZ, I am giving someone permission to have the same desires or do the same things I am doing.* Let me help you out, dear struggler. No! You're not. You don't have to give anyone permission to desire what you desire, do what you've done, or start doing what you're doing. They will do it on their own if they have the desire to do it. Yes, you may influence someone, even indirectly, but sin is always personal. It is a choice. It is a decision made by the one who was motivated or influenced or who arbitrarily decided to participate in a particular transaction. So, worry less about your silent wish of someone else to sin and purposefully decide how you will change the trajectory of your life with your decisions. You would be in a better position to influence positively when your lifestyle reflects what you say. Own your desires, your intentions, and your actions. Stop passing the buck around. It really stops with you.

I can still feel the reverberations of Jesus's rebuke to the unqualified religious leaders:

> Why do you look at the speck in your brother's eye, but fail to notice the beam in your own eye? How can you say to your brother, "Let me take the speck out of your eye" while there is still a beam in your own eye?" You hypocrite! First take the beam out of your own eye, and then you will see clearly to remove the speck from your brother's eye. (Matthew 7:3–5 KJV)

This instruction is empowering to the oppressed, and it is reenergizing to the demotivated truth-seeker who seemed to have experienced rejection from judgments served by unqualified others. The apostle James seals the gift with an instruction:

Make no mistake. The aim of confronting wrongdoing is always to restore the fallen.

My dear brothers and sisters, if someone among you wanders away from the truth and is brought back, you can be sure that whoever brings the sinner back from wandering will save that person from death and bring about the forgiveness of many sins. (James 5:19, 20 NLT)

Discovery 7

Persuading or influencing others against unhealthy spiritual living is falling short of "the mark of the high calling" in Jesus and is against the will of God. At some point, you were purposefully tempted by someone, but you have also intentionally challenged someone to resist your temptation. Regardless of what the individual's motivation was to tempt you, you either resisted or gracefully or desperately accepted the offer. You have had countless opportunities to present to others an agenda that was to your advantage and calculatedly so. The difference is that you may not have had the details of the temptation presented to you, but you did have the details of the temptation you presented to your target. Our motivations have not always been for the advantage of others. And when they appeared to be so, we usually have the patience to wait for our long-awaited benefits. Why? Every temptation has acceptance at its core.

Temptation because of its selfish motivation may not always be godly, morally supportive, virtuously elevating, or even congenial. One thing that is certain is its dazzling presentation and persuasive agenda. Although all temptations may not be demoralizing, they all seek to move an individual from cherished virtues to a point of uncertainty. Care should be exercised in the presentation of temptations that are inherently incongruent with spiritual virtues. To come dressed as an angel of light with malicious intentions is tantamount to deception and is rebellious against God's plan for someone's life. By so doing, the human tempter is joining ranks with the adversary of souls and fulfilling a deadly role. Yes, temptation is not sin, but tempting to sin is being rebellious and therefore sinful.

Discovery 8

Christianity is a naturally attractive context for temptation. Christianity is founded on the belief that Jesus, the only Son of God, was given to humankind through Mary, baptized by John the Baptist, his first cousin, tempted by Lucifer after He had fasted forty days and nights in the Arabian wilderness, lived and was betrayed and denied by two of his disciples, was rejected by those among whom he came, died for the salvation of the world (past, present, and future), resurrected three days after He was crucified by Roman soldiers, ascended to heaven, and promised His disciples that He will be back again. Christianity is built on the foundation that Jesus Christ was in all points tempted like we are being tempted, yet He did not sin. His life on this earth was demonstrative of the life expected of His disciples, including the evangelization of the world by His disciples.

Christianity promotes spiritually empowered living over temptations, love for enemies, monogamous marriages, and love for God and humanity. It is demonstrated through charitable giving, exemplary citizenry, and virtues such as kindness, mercy, forgiveness, and grace. All of what Christianity espouses argues the adversary is humanly distant and spiritually impossible.

They are impossible, and they have never been accomplished before by a mortal without a supernatural advantage.

The quest to overcome what is naturally possible for humankind is an impossible task and not at all enviable. Those who try to overcome what is natural for humans to do are seen as failures and otherworldly. The enemy of the soul presents all temptations as humankind's rightful benefits deprived by God. He presents God as unjust and exact in His judgments, which is the hallmark of all fear in the hearts of Christians.

"That Jesus was tempted to sin but did not sin," argues the enemy, "cannot be compared to humankind. He had an advantage, and I will prove that his expectations are unfair."

The controversy between good and evil will culminate with the Son of God being accounted righteous—not for His salvation but for justice displayed to the universe. Jesus Christ will be rightfully vindicated for making it possible for all to overcome willful sin in the flesh. The experience of Jesus in the wilderness manifested in his earthly ministry and gave Him the earthly experience to be touched with the feelings of our infirmities. He understands temptations in the flesh and in the spirit. He is qualified to be our High Priest (Hebrews. 4:15 AKJV).

Those who are seeking to journey with God need not trouble themselves with human flesh perfection. Human flesh perfection is an illusion, and performance to attain the same is a work of spiritual futility. All effort should be made to submit the will to God through His Son, Jesus Christ, the Substitute perfection for every sinner. God accepts the perfection of His Son Jesus on behalf of everyone who surrenders their sinful nature and sinfulness to him and accepts His perfect character.

No effort to submit to the will of God is useless for this should be our momentary effort. No amount of effort should be spared in doing so. What is useless, however, is the frustration of the heart to accumulate grace through good behavior. Anyone who seeks to establish their salvation relationship with God on the basis of their effort will fall short of the gift of salvation.

> For it is by grace you have been saved, through faith—and this is not from yourselves, it is the gift of God—not by works, so that no one can boast. (Ephesians 2:8, 9 NIV)

ASSESSMENT QUESTIONS

What temptation/s am I more susceptible to accept in my walk with God?

_____

_____

What makes me more susceptible to temptation/s?

_____

_____

Since my last temptation, can I confidently say that I have grown spiritually? If yes, in what way?

_____

_____

How do I prepare to resist temptations from the area/s of weakness in my life?

_____

_____

What area/s in my Christian experience have I left unguarded? Is it because I believe I have great spiritual advantage there—or because I believe those areas are not so significant?

_____

_____

How do I apply 1 Corinthians 10:12 to my life?

_____

_____

When last did I examine the desires of my heart?

_____

_____

Don't get fooled.
The adversary is
analytically punctual,
methodically
situational,
unconventionally
conventional, and
honorably
non-repulsive.
He comes disguised as
everything for which
we have ever wished.

CHAPTER 11

The Fear to Desire More

Delight thyself also in the Lord: and He shall give the desire of thine heart. Commit thy way unto the Lord; trust also in Him, and He shall bring it to pass.

—Psalm 37:4–5 (KJV)

Why do Seventh-day Adventists Christians always seem to be promoting poverty?" That's the question I asked my district pastor one day after he was through preaching about the rich young ruler (Matthew 19:16–22 AKJV). "Why is it that every time you preach about getting saved, you always mention that it is difficult for a rich man to enter heaven?"

> And again I say unto you, "It is easier for a camel to go through the eye of a needle, than for a rich man to enter into the kingdom of God." (Matthew 19:24 AKJV)

Why the emphasis? Are you saying something to us that we were not getting? Is there something wrong with a Christian desiring more? What should we desire as Christians? By the time he was through preaching that Sabbath morning, I was beginning to believe that God preferred to have Christians remain poor because the probability of them attaining salvation was certainly higher than for the one who possesses earthly wealth—and that God was displeased when we pay attention to desires outside of the spiritual desire to honor him.

Eligibility for salvation, I concluded, was a rejection of wealth, possessions, status, power, and prestige in all forms, at all levels, in all places, and for all purposes. Additionally, I concluded that an acceptance of meager means or poverty as a virtuous disposition demonstrable in hermit living and charity defendant, was the ideal for all who would make it to glory (heaven). That was my only interpretation of the sermon.

He was passionate about his presentation and persuasive in his application of the rich young ruler's lifestyle to modern-day Christianity. Needless to say, I was very troubled about the ideology then and more so now that I am a working adult with a family:

> And, behold, one came and said unto him, Good Master, what good thing shall I do, that I may have eternal life? And he said unto him, Why callest thou me good? There is none good but one, that is, God: but if thou wilt enter into life, keep the commandments. He saith unto him, Which? Jesus said, Thou shalt do no murder, Thou shalt not commit

adultery, Thou shalt not steal, Thou shalt not bear false witness, Honor thy father and thy mother: and, Thou shalt love thy neighbor as thyself. The young man saith unto him, All these things have I kept from my youth up: what lack I yet? Jesus said unto him, If thou wilt be perfect, go and sell that thou hast, and give to the poor, and thou shalt have treasure in heaven: and come and follow me. But when the young man heard that saying, he went away sorrowful: for he had great possessions." (Matthew 19:16–22 AKJV)

My issue was not the scriptural reference but the inferred preference for poverty or the minimal accumulation of wealth. My issue was the inference that less is better and that more or much more is bad. The disturbance I was having was the subtle distribution of the prescription for meager, the insinuation that the desire to have much was intertwined with the destructive element of guilt.

I am certain that two out of three believers have wrestled with the application of that narrative in their journeys with God. Should I want more than I have now? How much more should I want? If I do decide to accept that I want more, how will it impact my relationship with God? This is a legitimate series of questions. The struggle is a perennial one because success in earthly wealth is often regarded as evil.

I have discovered that the alternative to good is evil, that the opposite to much is little, that less than better is fair, that better than better is best, that the opposite to discipline is no discipline, that the alternative to success is failure, that the contradiction to growth is death, and that the antithesis to indecisiveness is purpose.

The single principle that runs through their core is desire. You either desire something and work toward achieving it—or you daydream about it and don't attain it. That struggle is the embodiment of success: to desire heart fulfillment. God desires that we win and that we prosper. How do I know? If you take time to understand the drive that propels you to want more and to get better, you will certainly discover that you are answering to the loud consciousness of God in your heart: "What does God want me to achieve? In what way must I use the potential that God has placed within me? Notwithstanding the limitations around me, how much must I achieve?

God desires
that we win.

The concept that God will supply all our needs is foreign to those who promote rugged individualism outside of God. As far as they are concerned, it is hard work that pays off and not God who gives. It is in those daily hours at school, the diligent work hours, the wise stock investments, and the prudential financial planning that resulted in their achievements and not God. It is not so. Human efforts combined with the resources supplied by God are rewarded, by God, to all who labor diligently. This should be the attitude of all believers because the belief that God is the Creator of all things lies at the heart of Christianity. The Christian remains cognizant of man's contribution in the journey of success and believes that it is "in Him (God) we live and move and have our being. As some of your own poets have said, 'We are his offspring'" Acts 17:28 (NIV). By so doing, we don't model the individualism of the world, but we model to the world how to acknowledge God's favor and provisions for His creation.

The Christian believer has needs like every other human being. Let's not drown that reality in the sea of myopia. The Christian believer does not possess immunity to the desires of wanting more out of life or the desire to accumulate wealth. The challenge, however, is the inability to establish balance in achievements and acknowledgment of God as the ultimate owner of all things. What some fear is their survivability if they were to commit themselves to discipleship in Jesus or acknowledge God as the owner of all things. They fear that they would constantly be in want and not be able to have a comfortable lifestyle stifles the very thing they so desire.

The fear of desiring has left many Christians discouraged. They fear that asking risks the possibility of not receiving, thus signaling a lack of faith. Further, to desire introduces the idea of selfishness. In the minds of many "to desire" is "to sin" and has therefore to be kept under subjection lest access is given to the adversary to occupy the heart, leading the soul to sin.

Wanting has also been given a negative label. To many, it infers a desire to have what God has not willed that we should have. If God wanted us to have it, then we would have had it. Scripture verses are often used to forward that argument. The verse states "For the Lord God is our sun and our shield. He gives us grace and glory. The Lord will withhold no good thing from those who do what is right" (Psalm 84:11 NLT).

Another frequently cited scripture reference is Psalm 37:4 (KJV): "Delight thyself also in the Lord: and he shall give thee (you) the desires of thine heart." It is therefore unprofitable to ask God for anything since the response is still arbitrarily His prerogative to give or not to give to anyone the desire of their hearts. Quite a gloomy perspective that is. Very desponding is this ideology to the most enthusiastic believing heart.

Desire is not synonymous with sin. Make no mistake in conflicting the two. Everyone desires one thing or another, at some time or another, even those things they may have been taught to shun. So, it is incorrect to conclude that desire causes sin. Desires metamorphosize when furnished with a decision to satisfy cravings:

> Sin results after a person is drawn after their own lusts and consumed by their desires. "Let no one say when he (she) is tempted, 'I am tempted by God,'" for God cannot be tempted by evil, nor does He Himself tempt anyone. But each one is tempted when he (she) is drawn away by his own desires and enticed. Then, when desire has conceived, it gives birth to sin; and sin, when it is full grown, brings forth death (James 1:13–15 NKJV)

To desire is to express humanity. Humanity comes out through the expression of desires.

Humankind is able to desire good or evil. Really, without the alternative, there would be stagnation of emotions, thoughts, and feelings. Humankind can desire success and not attain it. Mismanaged desires can significantly disrupt desired outcomes. The role of choice cannot be overemphasized. The desire to be able to choose should always be jealously guarded. Guard your desire for A or for B. Desire is embedded in the phenomenal attribute of choice. Unfortunately, many persons lack the courage to maximize opportunities presented to them because they lack the desire to take responsibility for their lives. They would prefer to pass on that responsibility to someone else. Inadvertently, they fail to realize that choice deferred is choice denied.

It is significant to note that desire is not inherently sinful or naturally destructive. To desire is to express humanity. To manage desire is to be disciplined. To be disciplined is to stay guarded against character improprieties and behavioral dysfunctions. Don't be afraid of desiring. Instead, use your choice to desire that which is noble and elevating to yourself and to your community.

King Solomon said, "Those who control their tongue will have a long life; opening your mouth can ruin everything" (Proverbs 13:3 NLT). He further compared self-control to military might: "Better to be slow to anger than to be a mighty warrior, and one who controls his temper is better than one who captures a city" (Proverbs 16:32 NET). Desire to possess self-control.

To desire is to express humanity. Humanity comes out through the expression of desires. Unique usage of the word desire is found in the Bible. The first place we find the word desire is in the fiasco following the disobedience of Adam and Eve to Yahweh when they partook of an experience that was forbidden to them. The immediate result was expulsion from the Garden of Eden, the only place they knew as home. Adam and Eve were sternly rebuked, their behavior was chastised, and their future was retrofitted to continuously remind them of the rebellious experience they acquiesced in their home.

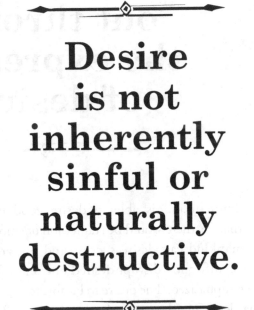

Desire is not inherently sinful or naturally destructive.

Yahweh said, "I will greatly multiply your sorrow and your conception; in sorrow you shall bring forth children; and your desire shall be to your husband, and he shall rule over you" (Genesis 3:16 KJV). "Your desire shall be to your husband," meaning הַקוּשָׁתֵ, from קוּשׁ to run, to have a vehement longing for a thing, to have a violent craving for a thing. The consistent interpretation here is that the determination of the woman's will, turnings, or inclinations shall be subjected or yielded to her husband.

The second place the word *desire* is used is in a completely different scenario between Cain and Abel in a falling out resulting from their attempt to please God.

> Then the Lord said to Cain, "Why are you angry? Why is your face downcast? If you do what is right, will you not be accepted? But if you do not do what is right, sin is crouching at your door; it desires to have you, but you must rule over it." (Genesis 4:6, 7 NIV)

Here we have an example of mismanaged desire that resulted in fateful sibling rivalry. In Genesis 4:8 (AKJV), we have the record of Cain, the elder brother, murdering his younger brother, Abel. This is a classic example of unbridled desire.

Scripture teaches the need for spiritual dependence on God for all our needs and not neglecting a physical engagement of our resources to reap the benefits of God's promises to us. Anything void of dependence on God implies humankind's self-sufficiency and independence from the Source of all life and Master of all creation. The concept of total dependence on God should not be seen as a laissez-faire approach or a debilitating syndrome of humankind's potential. Rather, it is an acknowledgement of who God is and His capacity to unlimitedly provide for all. Fear of God must not be allowed to stand in the way of our blessings from Him.

Fear of being disappointed by God led Cain to hate his younger brother. Angered over self-inflicted results motivated the evil desire that raised its hand against the innocent brother. We can learn from this account the fundamental principle in desiring. The desire, preoccupied with self, presents the danger of inflicting pain on others, particularly if it is perceived that we are being obstructed. Care must be taken to reassess the motive of all desires. By doing so, we demonstrate compassion for ourselves and others.

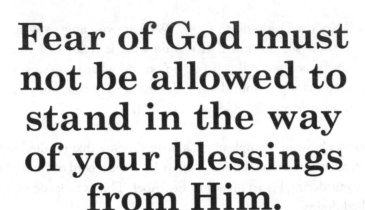

Fear of God must not be allowed to stand in the way of your blessings from Him.

Here are some empowering and defining applications of desiring more:

Sarai longed for a son. Yahweh's clock was differently timed from her biological clock. She functioned on human time, and He functioned on divine time. His thoughts are higher than her thoughts, and His ways are higher than her ways. Her plan to satisfy her desire procured a plan outside of Yahweh's plan and resulted in her chagrin and guilt:

> Now Sarai, Abram's wife, had borne him no children. But she had an Egyptian slave named Hagar; so she said to Abram, "The Lord has kept me from having children. Go, sleep with my slave; perhaps I can build a family through her." Abram agreed to what Sarai said. So after Abram had been living in Canaan ten years, Sarai his wife took her Egyptian slave Hagar and gave her to her husband to be his wife. He slept with Hagar, and she conceived. When she knew she was pregnant, she began to despise her mistress. Then Sarai said to Abram, "You are responsible for the wrong I am suffering. I put my slave in your arms, and now that she knows she is pregnant, she

despises me. May the Lord judge between you and me.
(Genesis 16:1–5 NIV)

Yahweh responded to her desire and blessed her with Isaac in her senior years. I like how she responded when told that her long dreamed dream would come true:

> So she laughed silently to herself and said, "How could a worn-out woman like me enjoy such pleasure, especially when my master—my husband—is also so old?" Then the Lord said to Abraham, "Why did Sarah laugh? Why did she say, 'Can an old woman like me have a baby?' Is anything too hard for the Lord? I will return about this time next year, and Sarah will have a son."
> (Genesis 18: 12–14 NIV)

I am not sure if you have discovered that God's timing is always perfect and that His acts are always packaged with a deliverance blessing. In Sarah's case, God delivered her from community shame and established her generation through the son of her womb. God's timing is always able to reverse the ordinary, outperform the natural, make limitless the limited, restore the broken, uplift the downtrodden, exalt the rejected, establish the committed, defend the defenseless, provide shelter for the homeless, anoint the faithful, assign the undesignated, and remain merciful to the merciful and the merciless. God moves in the presence of disbelief when the heart is in covenant with Him. Yahweh is a covenant God:

> Abraham desired obedience to Yahweh's command than the physical salvation of his promised son, Isaac. The biblical account reads: Some time later, God tested Abraham's faith. "Abraham!" God called."
> Yes," he replied. "Here I am."
> "Take your son, your only son—yes, Isaac, whom you love so much—and go to the land of Moriah. Go and sacrifice him as a burnt offering on one of the mountains, which I will show you."

The next morning Abraham got up early. He saddled his donkey and took two of his servants with him, along with his son, Isaac. Then he chopped wood for a fire for a burnt offering and set out for the place God had told him about. On the third day of their journey, Abraham looked up and saw the place in the distance. "Stay here with the donkey," Abraham told the servants. "The boy and I will travel a little farther. We will worship there, and then we will come right back." So Abraham placed the wood for the burnt offering on Isaac's shoulders, while he himself carried the fire and the knife. As the two of them walked on together, Isaac turned to Abraham and said, "Father?" "Yes, my son?" Abraham replied. "We have the fire and the wood," the boy said, "but where is the sheep for the burnt offering?" "God will provide a sheep for the burnt offering, my son," Abraham answered. And they both walked on together. When they arrived at the place where God had told him to go, Abraham built an altar and arranged the wood on it. Then he tied his son, Isaac, and laid him on the altar on top of the wood. And Abraham picked up the knife to kill his son as a sacrifice. At that moment the angel of the Lord called to him from heaven, "Abraham! Abraham!" "Yes," Abraham replied. "Here I am!" "Don't lay a hand on the boy!" the angel said. "Do not hurt him in any way, for now I know that you truly fear God. You have not withheld from me even your son, your only son." (Genesis 22:1–12 NLT)

Rachel desired death if she won't have her craving for a son satisfied from her husband Jacob.

When Rachel saw that she was not bearing Jacob any children, she became jealous of her sister. So she said to Jacob, "Give me children, or I'll die!" (Genesis 30:1 NIV)

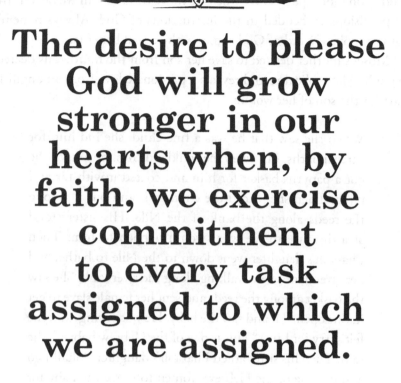

The desire to please God will grow stronger in our hearts when, by faith, we exercise commitment to every task assigned to which we are assigned.

The desire to please God will grow stronger in our hearts when, by faith, we exercise commitment to every task assigned to which we are assigned. No one is to live in the fantasy that unbelief will suddenly dissipate at a particular time, in a uniquely designated place, or under a supernatural cloud of circumstances, all will suddenly become well with their souls. No such cloud will appear to overshadow unbelief. No such cloud exists. No opportunities like this will show.

It is in the demonstration of small duties and unflattering efforts that we exhibit the courage to move unflinchingly forward to great attainments. It is through deliberate commitment and the application of our will to esteemed virtues and spiritual ideals that we will reach the zenith, thereby securing the fortitudinous character to survive uncharted waters. No tasks assigned, no responsibility given, no path directed is to be interpreted as an error on God's part. Only when we move by faith will we benefit from the provisions embedded in the instructions of God. Always remember that the spoken Word of God comes with eternal benefits.

Moses's mother desired to save her son from the murderous decree of Pharaoh. The biblical record reveals a passionate love from an anguished heart for the son of her womb:

> When she saw that he was a fine child, she hid him for three months. But when she could hide him no longer, she got a papyrus basket for him and coated it with tar and pitch. Then she placed the child in it and put it among the reeds along the bank of the Nile. His sister stood at a distance to see what would happen to him. Then Pharaoh's daughter went down to the Nile to bathe, and her attendants were walking along the riverbank. She saw the basket among the reeds and sent her female slave to get it. She opened it and saw the baby. He was crying, and she felt sorry for him. "This is one of the Hebrew babies," she said. Then his sister asked Pharaoh's daughter, "Shall I go and get one of the Hebrew women to nurse the baby for you?" Yes, go," she answered. So the girl went and got the baby's mother. Pharaoh's daughter said to her, "Take this baby and nurse him for me, and I will pay you." So the woman took the baby and nursed him. When the child grew older, she took him to Pharaoh's daughter and he became her son. She named him Moses, saying, "I drew him out of the water." (Exodus 2:1–10 NIV)

Jochebed's desire to save her son was demonstrated in getting him to the Nile River, which was an attraction site for many great Egyptians. The alacrity and alertness of a caring sister supported the family's plan to save their son and brother. The rescue benefited Jochebed's son in name, provision, and position. Yahweh's hands guided the dial that gave time, opportunity, salvation, and experience to Moses, Pharaoh's daughter's adopted son. He is still revered as one of the greats to walk the Earth.

Moses desired to experience God's physical glory. Here is another example of the innermost cravings in our spiritual lives. The desire for piety overrides the passionate embrace of empty religious traditions that carry form but very little, if any, appreciable substance.

> And Moses said, "Show me your glory." And the Lord said, "I will make all my goodness pass before your face, and I will proclaim the Lord by name before you; I will be gracious to whom I will be gracious, I will show mercy to whom I will show mercy." But he added, "You cannot see my face, for no one can see me and live." The Lord said, "Here is a place by me; you will station yourself on a rock. When my glory passes by, I will put you in a cleft in the rock and will cover you with my hand while I pass by. Then I will take away my hand, and you will see my back, but my face must not be seen." (Exodus 33:18–23 NET)

The desire for deep piety is not so much an intellectual exercise, as it is the discipline and application of the will to accept and appreciate biblical values. To desire godliness is markedly different from desiring a human relationship. Piety must be pursued. Time must be made for the subjection of the soul to the principles that will motivate its transformation. The navigation of fear in this regard is almost a nonissue because to know God is to spend time with Him. To spend time with God is to disavow every fearful doubt that the adversary may want to introduce in the heart. Moses discovered who Yahweh is because he was unafraid to be Moses with Him.

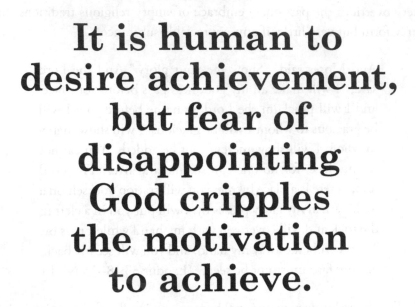

It is human to desire achievement, but fear of disappointing God cripples the motivation to achieve.

Caleb desired his dream inheritance:

> Now therefore give me this mountain, whereof the Lord spake in that day; for thou heardest in that day how the Anakims were there, and that the cities were great and fenced: if so be the Lord will be with me, then I shall be able to drive them out, as the Lord said. And Joshua blessed him, and gave unto Caleb the son of Jephunneh Hebron for an inheritance. Hebron therefore became the inheritance of Caleb the son of Jephunneh the Kenezite unto this day, because that he wholly followed the Lord God of Israel. And the name of Hebron before was Kirjath-arba; which Arba was a great man among the Anakims. And the land had rest from war. (Joshua 14:12–15 AKJV)

Desire, when disciplined, is indefatigable. The ability to differentiate its principles from moodiness and unbridled greed will motivate the dreamer to stay true to that dream, whatever it is. Desire, when disciplined, will propel the dreamer's conviction of duty, will motivate tenacity that interprets detours as opportunities for distraction, and with greater resoluteness see every detour as a reason for re-energization.

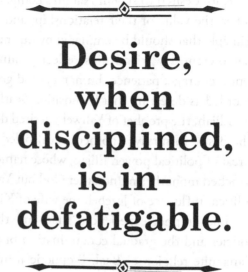

Desire, when disciplined, is in-defatigable.

Caleb demonstrated a dogged fixation on a forty-year-old dream that would not leave his memory throughout his understudy of Joshua. He was cognizant of its history, knowledgeable of its challenges, was nonetheless committed to his gains despite all existing anomalies. Oh, the power of a dream!

Ruth desired the companionship and friendship of Naomi. Friendship matters! Ruth discovered that a commitment to friendship runs deeper than mere emotions, taller than myths, and wider than empty impressions. In the face of adversity, death, starvation, and emotional distress, Ruth expressed heartfelt appreciation to her "once-upon-a-time mother-in-law, Naomi. I continue to marvel at the boldness of Ruth's request.

It is human to desire achievement, yet fear of disappointing God cripples the motivation to achieve. Ruth 1:16–18 (NLT) says:

> But Ruth replied, "Don't ask me to leave you and turn back. Wherever you go, I will go; wherever you live, I will live. Your people will be my people, and your God will be my God. Wherever you die, I will die, and there I will be buried. May the Lord punish me severely if I allow anything but death to separate us!" When Naomi

saw that Ruth was determined to go with her, she said nothing more.

Ruth desired to stay in Naomi's company because of who Naomi was to her, the value of their relationship, and what it represented. This is a principle that should be emulated by our modern society. It is significant that present-day friendships reflect genuineness, formidable character, depth, courage, patience, humanity, and godliness. Nothing but death is recorded as defeating that friendship. Death was only a divider.

Elijah, the prophet of Yahweh, desired death for fear of Queen Jezebel. The desire to survive another ordeal paled in the face of the terrorizing threat of political power. Elijah, whose name means "Yahweh is my God," preached monotheism (no other God but Yahweh) and grew fearful of the political influence of Jezebel, the wife of King Ahab.

The prophet experienced firsthand the intensification of Jezebel's policies and the gradual contamination of the religion of Yahweh by the Canaanite religion of Baal. Prophetic ministry, as Elijah understood it, was over when Queen Jezebel threatened to take his life. Physically alone, emotionally drained, without institutional representation, depressed, and self-isolated, he lamented the prophetic passion that once exuded the plains of Israel's northern kingdom where he served. No longer excited under the threat of death, the dark cloud of depression enveloped the demotivated prophet. "I am the only one left, and now they are trying to kill me too" (1 Kings 18:19–19:3 NIV). Elijah's desire conflicted with his purpose. He chose death over purpose. Yahweh resurrected Elijah from his prophetic grave.

Captain Naaman desired to be healed of his skin disease (2 Kings 5:1–19 AKJV). He expended all available resources to get to the one who he thought was the source of his healing. Reality set in when he was directed to the Jordan River to dip himself seven times. With much apprehension about the location and method of healing, Naaman hesitated to carry out the instruction of the prophet Elijah. His reluctance was short-lived as he was persuaded to obedience by an immediate community of subservient supporters. Naaman's desire to be healed battled with the prideful hesitation that enveloped his mind. The will overpowered the temporary disappointment and resulted in the most favorable outcome of his life. If your desire is to be healed of a malady, that same Source of healing is still available today. Yahweh is the God of unlimited means.

David desired the opportunity to defeat the Philistine giant, Goliath (1 Samuel 17 AKJV). David, the shepherd boy, understood purpose and benefit in the elimination of the oppositions symbolized in the person of Goliath. He developed and demonstrated unwavering courage and commitment to the cause he found justifiable.

David was motivated by the cause. The insults of the unbelieving to the God he served were greater motivation to defeat the adversary than any reward the community may have offered him in lieu of the potential victory. "I'm doing this for Jehovah! Let me physically go and silence the dissenting voice of the profligate."

The cause fueled his desire. David asked, "Is there not a cause?" Let me help you translate the question: "Have you understood the reason why we must defeat this giant and all that he represents?"

What is the motivation for the goals you have set out to achieve? Are the outcomes personal or communal? If they are communal, are you sufficiently motivated to pursue those goals even if the identical community continues to question your motivation?

Esther, the Persian queen, demonstrated an unusual commitment to the salvation of her Jewish people (Esther 4:16 NIV). The desire to stop a massacre was greater than any possible punishment the king could have pronounced on her life. Community service was greater than personal gain. Esther understood that "queenship" was resultant of community and therefore expendable in light of the greater good. Very strikingly reverberates the conscientious assessment of her relevant and anointed relative Mordecai, in the revelation of her purpose:

> If you keep quiet at this time, liberation and protection for the Jews will appear from another source, while you and your father's household perish. It may very well be that you have achieved royal status for such a time as this! (Esther 4:14 NET)

With sterling courage, Esther's response was heartily adequate. "Go, gather together all the Jews who are in

Susa, and fast for me. Do not eat or drink for three days, night or day. I and my attendants will fast as you do. When this is done, I will go to the king, even though it is against the law. And if I perish, I perish." (Esther 4:16 NIV)

Peter desired and walked on water (Matthew 14:22, 23 AKJV). The Gospel writers present Peter, Jesus's disciple, as a desirer of a deeper friend, a companion, and a defender of Jesus Christ. All of the experiences that Peter had with Jesus during His earthly ministry were transformative. However, I wish to highlight Peter's desire to step out of his secure place to step on water to go to Jesus. He asked for more. He asked for different. He asked for the unusual. Peter asked for a new experience. One of the many lessons in that account is that we should only desire more when what you possess is less than your promise. Peter had experienced the power of God many times before, and now felt ready to risk taking the chance to experience more.

Abrasive as his disposition may have been interpreted at different moments in his life, Peter desired to be with Jesus more than many who had been around him. Peter understood the dangers of getting out of the boat to do something that he had not done before. He desired more. Peter spoke for more. He asked for more. Peter acted for more. He challenged his faith and doubts for more. Peter stepped out for more. He endangered his life for more. Peter displayed no fear for the countless possibilities. He was confident that he would be safe with Jesus. One of the dangers of staying in our comfort zones is that we will continue to miss the manifestations of God's power in our lives because we fear the unknown.

Only desire more when what you possess is less than your promise.

Desire Myth Busters

Myth	Myth Buster
To want more out of life is to become worldly, greedy, and pleasurable.	Not true. We have been commanded in Ecclesiastes 9:10 (NLT): "Whatever you do, do well. For when you go to the grave, there will be no work or planning or knowledge or wisdom." Further, the scripture teaches that we are to use the times of plenty to prepare for the lean times. "He becometh poor that dealeth with a slack hand: but the hand of the diligent maketh rich; He that gathereth in summer is a wise son: but he that sleepeth in harvest is a son that causeth shame" (Proverbs 10:4, 5 AKJV).

Money is evil.	Not true! For the love of money is a root of all kinds of evil. Some people, eager for money, have wandered from the faith and pierced themselves with many griefs (1 Timothy 6:10 NIV).
God is not in the business of giving wealth. His blessings don't promote wealth.	Not True! God grants blessings and special favors to those who desire to give service and not self-gratification: "The Lord was pleased that Solomon had asked for wisdom. So God replied,"Because you have asked for wisdom in governing my people with justice and have not asked for a long life or wealth or the death of your enemies—I will give you what you asked for! I will give you a wise and understanding heart such as no one else has had or ever will have! And I will also give you what you did not ask for—riches and fame! No other king in all the world will be compared to you for the rest of your life! And if you follow me and obey my decrees and my commands as your father, David, did, I will give you a long life'" (1 Kings 3:10–14 NLT). The blessing of the Lord brings wealth, without painful toil for it (Proverbs 10:22 NIV).
We should worry about our needs because no one else will do it for us.	The need to labor for the things we need cannot be overemphasized. However, we need never to forget that our Father, the Creator of this and other worlds, has made provision for us to have everything we need. "That is why I tell you not to worry about everyday life—whether you have enough food and drink, or enough clothes to wear. Isn't life more than food, and your body more than clothing? Look at the birds. They don't plant or harvest or store food in barns, for your heavenly Father feeds them. And aren't you far more valuable to him than they are? Can all your worries add a single moment to your life?

	And why worry about your clothing? Look at the lilies of the field and how they grow. They don't work or make their clothing, yet Solomon in all his glory was not dressed as beautifully as they are. And if God cares so wonderfully for wildflowers that are here today and thrown into the fire tomorrow, he will certainly care for you. Why do you have so little faith? So don't worry about these things, saying, 'What will we eat? What will we drink? What will we wear?' These things dominate the thoughts of unbelievers, but your heavenly Father already knows all your needs. Seek the kingdom of God above all else, and live righteously, and he will give you everything you need. So don't worry about tomorrow, for tomorrow will bring its own worries. Today's trouble is enough for today" (Matthew 6:25–34 NLT).
God is too busy with the affairs of this world to care about me.	The eyes of the Lord are upon the righteous, and his ears are open unto their cry (Psalm 34:15 KJV). The righteous will not beg (Psalm 37:25 KJV).
Working demonstrates a lack of faith in God. He will give to us what we need.	There is dignity in labor. Slothfulness and laziness must be rebuked. It is a disgrace to live parasitically when we have the capacity to labor and to increase the availability of resources for ourselves and those around us.
All we need are the basics. Nothing more.	God's promise to you and me is that our needs will be met. "And my God will meet all your needs according to the riches of his glory in Christ Jesus" (Philippians 4:19 NIV).

ASSESSMENT QUESTIONS

What is/are my desire/s?

_____

_____

How is/are that/those desire/s in sync with my walk with God?

_____

_____

How have I nurtured it/them?

_____

_____

Understanding it is never wrong to openly share with God the contents of my heart, have I shared that/those desire/s with Him?

_____

_____

What meaning, if any, have you attached to that/those desire/s?

_____

_____

Consider what it would be to compare present desire/s with an/other alternative/s. What does my life picture look like?

_____

_____

In the past week, how has my passion for living gotten drawn into that/those desires? Am I anxious about satisfying it/them?

_____

_____

What if now were my only opportunity to change my world, would I meet the standard?

CHAPTER 12

The Fear of Apostasy

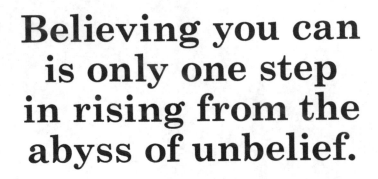

Believing you can is only one step in rising from the abyss of unbelief.

High church dropouts! Nomads! Revolving front doors! Banging back doors! Negative perceptions! Prodigals and degenerates. Many are grief-stricken over what appears to be a perennial issue and a recipe for spiritual discouragement in Christianity's apparent failure to soundly attract millennials, its inconsistency in building relationships, and the whitewashing of biblical doctrines.

Christians historically have been afraid of apostatizing. Proverbs 26:11 serves as a rebuke to the mere thought of reneging on a previously professed faith. No one wants to be the proverbial dog that returns to its vomit or be considered foolish for returning to a former lifestyle:

Like a dog that returns to its vomit is a fool who reverts to his folly. (NRSV)

Judgment is pronounced in 2 Peter 2:20–22 (BSB) presenting quite a somber description of those who renounce their faith or reconnect with heretical beliefs:

> If indeed they have escaped the corruption of the world through the knowledge of our Lord and Savior Jesus Christ, only to be entangled and overcome by it again, their final condition is worse than it was at first. It would have been better for them not to have known the way of righteousness than to have known it and then to turn away from the holy commandment passed on to them. Of them the proverbs are true: "A dog returns to its vomit," and, "A sow that is washed goes back to her wallowing in the mud."

This further exacerbates the fear of those despairing over their salvation. Am I saved? Will I be saved? What must I do to be saved? Am I in the faith of Jesus Christ—or am I tolerating a system of beliefs that I no longer support? Backsliders are confused about spiritual restoration, heretics are troubled by their theological positions, and apostates are committed to the rejection of Christianity. All of that is in the quest for a deep, relevant, satisfying, pragmatic, and otherworldly spiritual piety. The void created by "the usual" has left many believers destitute and in search for "the relevant."

I was conducting a revival series at a popular church.

At the close of the Friday night service, a young lady came to me in tears and said, "Pastor, may I speak to you?"

I escorted her aside in order to talk.

As she looked into my face with agony, she said, "Your appeal tonight brought me to my knees in tears. You don't know, but I accepted Jesus as my personal Savior some years ago, and I was about as honest about it as I knew how to be. I was studying the Bible, praying, and having a wonderful time serving the Lord. I was happy and found meaning in life for the first time in a long while. Shortly afterward, I went off to college and participated in spiritual activities. I also aligned myself with a particular group that led me down a path where serving the Lord was no longer enjoyable. I no longer had the assurance of salvation in my heart. I am visiting here on vacation. I was invited here by my friend, but we're leaving early next week for college. I heard you speak on the prodigal Christian tonight. I'm struggling. You said there is still hope, but you don't know what I've done. I listened to a preacher speak on apostasy, and he said if you ever leave Christ and go back into sin, you are eternally lost." At that point, she looked directly into my eyes and asked, "Pastor, is there hope for me? Can I be restored? Am I lost forever?

Before I could have responded, with a smile on her face, she said, "If there is, I need to be restored through water baptism."

I felt spiritually revived as I listened to the heartfelt cry of that daughter of God. With affirmation and conviction in my heart, I said, "The Holy Spirit led you to this place tonight to renew your walk with God. You cannot change your past, and your present is much too heavy for you. Surrender to Jesus the burden you are now carrying, and your future will be happy."

We confirmed her path to spiritual restoration and thanked God in prayer for her deliverance. The following day, she renewed her walk with God in baptism.

Although not often admitted, the fear of being eternally lost is a real nightmare for many Christians. This should not be dealt with glibly. It is troubling that many are hesitant to ask questions that can very well help to deepen their faith, but they are afraid that if they ask, it will be interpreted by many as a departure from traditionally held beliefs and practices and thus a path to spiritual apathy. There is a need to differentiate apostasy from heresy because there is a distinction.

Apostasy and Heresy

We will use two instruments to incisively establish the differences needed to move forward. The first instrument is church tradition. In religious terms, heresy is commonly understood to be a deviation from, or falsification of, biblical truth. To be considered heretical presupposes that a biblical body of truth is valid for all and that no one has the right or authority to alter it. That presupposition further assumes that there is a criterion to distinguish truth from its falsification or deviation.

Historically, only the teaching ministry of the Christian church was credited with the authority to interpret and establish truth from error. That exclusivity, through its religious leaders, consequently made pronouncements about what was truth or heretical. Protestant reformers rejected that understanding. The second instrument is scripture. Protestant Christians accept and promote the Bible as the only and exclusive instrument by which truth is defined and falsehood identified.

Apostasy incorporates the view of heresy, but it points to the time when intensity and radicalization of falsification led an individual to abandon and fully separate themselves from biblical truth and from Christ as the truth. In some cases, there is a precipitous drop in faith. In others, there is a gradual falling away from the truth and from God's saving grace. Apostasy, therefore, is never sudden. It happens over time.

Apostasy, as a behavior, is the cumulative result of a flawed walk with God. That walk was inundated with unexplainable periods when the glorified idea of God's presence, wisdom, and power were conceptually and experientially not evident in the life of the believer. Apostasy, as a concept, is a failed attempt to substantiate, through philosophical means, the idea of God's presence, wisdom, and power. The latter is a state of spiritual defection from biblical truth, and the former is a reaction to an existing spiritual dilemma.

Backsliding

Backsliding is a spiritual condition that results from spiritual apathy or disregard for the things of God, whether on the part of an individual or a community of believers bonded by a prior covenantal pledge of commitment to uphold the doctrine and commandments of the Lord. Backsliding includes active departure from a practical confession of faith and from the ethical standards prescribed for God's people in the scriptures.

To varying degrees, depending on the severity of the spiritual apathy, including public disregard for God and His commandments, the spiritually wayward experience a season of estrangement and abandonment from

God and His people. God's displeasure with spiritual waywardness was demonstrative in the lives of physical Israel, resulting in Babylonian exile. The prophet Hosea describes Israel in unsavory terms as an adulterous people. Israel, here, was depicted as spiritually immoral, adulterous, depraved, and profane in the name of God. Despite their spiritual condition, they would refuse the invitation to walk in the grace of God. That stubbornness of heart, unfaithfulness, waywardness, and other manifestations of constant refusal of God's call to repentance through the power of the Holy Spirit will seal the heart of the backslider in spiritual apostasy.

> Their mother is a shameless prostitute and became pregnant in a shameful way. She said, "I'll run after other lovers and sell myself to them for food and water, for clothing of wool and linen, and for olive oil and drinks." (Hosea 2:5 NLT)

> They ask a piece of wood for advice! They think a stick can tell them the future! Longing after idols has made them foolish. They have played the prostitute, serving other gods and deserting their God. (Hosea 4:12 NLT)

> They have betrayed the honor of the Lord, bearing children that are not his. Now their false religion will devour them along with their wealth. (Hosea 5:7 NLT)

Some are quick to judge and compare the conversion of others in their walks with God. This must be avoided at all costs. Jesus Christ is our only Standard Bearer and not our fellow brother or sister. Our interests should be to aspire to the earthly spiritual maturity of Jesus since He accounts for our imperfection with His perfection. We encourage each other to pursue the standard as prescribed in the scriptures.

We may have spiritual parents, mentors, and teachers who guide us in the faith, but we have to remember that our salvation resides in God alone. Many will fall away in the end-times, including some people who we revere as strong Christians of great faith. We should never establish ourselves as standard bearers of God's character. Instead, we should exhort the power of God through His Son, Jesus Christ, to keep us from falling. When we recognize our heartfelt responses to the saving position of Christ, we can say, "Follow my example, as I follow the example of Christ" (1 Corinthians 11:1 NIV).

No one is immune to the possibility of apostatizing. Anyone can commit the sin of apostasy, but the grace of God makes the difference. One must replace any sense of self-worthiness and self-stability with God's grace and stability. This requires spiritual commitment to Bible study, prayer, and soul examination. The apostle Paul gave this prescription:

> Examine yourselves to see whether you are in the faith; test yourselves. Do you not realize that Christ Jesus is in you—unless, of course, you fail the test? (2 Corinthians 13:5 NIV)

It was a problem in the early Christian church, and it is still a problem today. In John 6:60–66 (AKJV), the Gospel writer gave examples of many disciples who abandoned Jesus because the philosophy of His kingdom was incongruent with their political agendas. In Galatians 1:6 (AKJV), we have another example of apostasy. Christian believers rejected Jesus Christ and their faith. It was also prophesied that apostasy will be a sign of the end-times before the earthly return of Jesus.

In 1 Timothy 4:1 (AKJV), the apostle showed that many will fall away in the end-times, going after the teachings of demons:

> Now the Spirit speaketh expressly, that in the latter times some shall depart from the faith, giving heed to seducing spirits, and doctrines of devils.

Erroneous teachings can cause Christians to fall away from our faith:

> Ye therefore, beloved, seeing ye know these things before, beware lest ye also, being led away with the error of the wicked, fall from your own steadfastness. (2 Peter 3:17 AKJV)

Therefore, dear friends, since you have been forewarned, be on your guard that you do not get led astray by the error of these unprincipled men and fall from your firm grasp on the truth. (2 Peter 3:17 NET)

Apostasy is a stigma that every Christian fear. However, not every Christian will reflect sameness in their explanations of their walks with God. What then should be the identity of the ones who have grown to know God differently from what they have been taught? In Matthew 7 (AKJV), Jesus asks that we guard against the propensity to judge and pass judgment on others.

I was invited to speak to a classroom of students as they were preparing for an examination. As I walked into the setting, I sensed anxiety, ambivalence, confusion, and fear. The looks on the faces of the teachers spoke volumes, reflecting much of what the students exhibited.

This is troubling, I thought. *What am I expected to do when the outspoken presence of anxiety is so evident in the same room with me? Am I supposed to work a miracle here?*

The atmosphere was conducive for a clinical psychotherapist, pastor, motivational speaker, life coach, husband, father, son, or marriage officer. For the clinical psychotherapist, there was need to address anxiety, depression, fear, and other raging emotions. For the pastor, since the gathering was in a church, the mood was just right for exorcizing whatever level of evil gripped the atmosphere. For the motivational speaker, the negative energies, if sustained, would undermine the foundation of whatever level of future successes those students might have. For the life coach, fear needed to be demystified. For the husband, the future of those young people could not have been left to chance with a negative relationship. For the father, the philosophy of rewarding a laissez-faire attitude needed to be extracted from those impressionable young minds. For the son, the idea of seeing siblings marginalized because of unimproved opportunities confronted the core of my life's principles. For the marriage officer, there was immediate motivation to fast-track the inevitable divorce between success and a lack of discipline.

Everything went well until the breakout session. I asked, "Would you like me to pray as we close?"

The student's response jolted me for a moment. "I don't like talking about God."

I said, "Are you a Christian?"

"Well, I come to church with my grandparent. She's an administrator of the church."

"Do you pray at home?"

"I pray when my grandparent prays, but I don't pray outside of that. I just don't like to talk about God. What I want is to go live with my mother."

Realizing the disconnect between my desire to pray with the student and her refusal to talk to God, I mustered the courage and asked, "So, is there anything you would like me to present to God in prayer on your behalf?"

"No," she replied. "I don't want to pray."

At that point, and with the impressive inflection in her voice, I conceded.

That account is not unique. It is representative of many who have issues with "the God thing." Some persons gravitate to God, and others move away from Him. We have established that many serve God out of fear of eternal damnation. Others remain in communities where the tradition of worshipping God has been normalized to feel a stronger pull to religiosity because of the religious environment.

In some cases, a relationship with God is measured by an immersion of oneself in religious activities, including regular donations to charitable organizations. In others, performing rites and animal sacrifices are the norms of spiritual expression. As spiritually charging as those experiences may be, one may participate in all of them and still not have the conviction of God in their personal life. The knowledge and acceptance of God is the compelling qualifier of discipleship. It is built on the spiritual foundation of faith. Faith becomes the platform from which all manifestations of God are explained and doctrinal beliefs established, resulting in loyalty to both God and religious faith. A rejection or defection from those established beliefs would be considered heretical and detrimental to the soundness of one's spiritual development.

The fear of apostasy is real. That fear needs to be analyzed from two angles. The first is fear that my present beliefs conflict with my conviction and that I no longer believe what I used to believe; therefore, I need to be true to my conscience. The second is fear of knowing that I have apostatized and am in danger of eternal damnation. The consequences of apostatizing may be the fear that many harbor, and it is be expressed as the reason for silencing the conscience when deciding the way forward from presently held beliefs. In either of these scenarios, fear dominates the relationship and stifles the spiritual growth of the believer.

The fear of apostasy may be linked to denominational traditions established on philosophical biblical extrapolations and not on biblical positions for salvation in Jesus Christ. For many, the struggle is denominational traditions versus biblical teachings on conversion. Inkye's experience with his home church would be a classic example of this behavior.

Inkye was an active youth ministries leader at his church. He led the music department. During his sophomore year of college, he became convinced that wearing cosmetic jewelry was not sinful. Abstaining from cosmetic jewelry was only a lifestyle standard that was promoted by his denomination to authenticate outward representation of a spiritual conversion. Because of his need to be true to his conscience, he wore a necklace to choir rehearsal on a Friday night for the first time since becoming a baptized member of that congregation. Inkye was frowned upon at rehearsal by the choir director.

He disregarded the behavior as a mistake or a heightened sense of expectation. Inkye's new appearance was questioned at church the next day. The youth pastor cited inappropriateness and disregard for the doctrines of the church. Inkye, despite the reprimand, continued to attend church services, but he would leave the necklace covered beneath his collar. On weekdays, however, Inkye would be seen wearing a necklace. He was cautioned about the apostate look and its impact on his walk with God. Later that year, at election of officers, Inkye was not returned as head of the music department of his church.

The struggle is reflective of existing realties in many Christian churches. What is unto salvation, and what is not? Inkye is among many who struggle with their belief in God vis-à-vis how they represent their religious organizations. There seem to be a faction that promotes liberty in

Christ and another that waves the Ten Commandments like a flag above the head of every other person they meet.

Because of the level of shame experienced from disclosing unpopular beliefs or convictions, many Christians suffer spiritual injustices at the hands of their fellow parishioners. It is sad but expected because conviction cannot be stopped. An idea planted in the heart will flourish and bear much fruit. If you have a conviction that is different from your previously held beliefs, and you still want to maintain membership with a particular church community or group of people, you are ethically bound to be true to yourself and to that community. They have a right to expect you to possess their spiritual convictions. It's only fair that it is so. However, knowing the nature of your community of interests and your need to be true to your conscience, your membership in any group with contrary views will need to be managed.

The fear of apostasy is also linked to the idea that every Christian believer has to reflect the same theological position on matters of spirituality. That idea finds much traction in fundamentalist traditions where membership in the church is confirmed by acceptance of—and adherence to—denominational beliefs. Although the idea is not unique to the church structure, as other organizations promote sameness in ideology, it has historically been used to highlight morality and character flaws in those with contrary convictions. Sameness has its place, but it should not be used to exalt the self above others. Loving the unbelieving is the key to the salvation of souls.

Some years ago, I visited a family who had once been members of a particular church. I couldn't understand why they had left or what motivated them to stay away from what seemed to be a warm church family atmosphere. The primary goal of my visit was to convince them to return to the fellowship. I was prepared to present them with a conversion message because I could not bear to see them leave.

During the visit, the family respectfully explained that they still love God, still believed in His plan of salvation for humankind, still believed that their sins had been paid for with the atoning blood of Jesus Christ, still believed in the weekly observance of the seventh-day Sabbath, the priestly ministry of Jesus Christ in the Heavenly sanctuary, still believed in respecting their body as a temple of the Holy Spirit, the spirit of prophecy and also believe in the second visible return of Jesus. However, they now believed the Seventh-day Adventist Church has lost the urgency of its message, has forgotten its mission and therefore unable to preach present truth, which is the only message for this time. They explained their belief on the theological compromises of the church with the papacy and the papacy's access to the membership and administration of the church organization. Consequently, they no longer wished to have any part in an apostate church. Further discussion led to their understanding of what they referred to as "present truth" and the third angel's message as revealed through the apocalyptic writing of the apostle John and the writings of Ellen G. White. Regrettably, my attempt to have them return to fellowship with the church was unsuccessful. It was very apparent that the fear of being labeled apostate did not sway the hurting family. What was strikingly glaring to me was the forwardness of the group to point out the moral and doctrinal flaws in their previous congregation, and the supposedly cavalier attitude of the church in handling issues that were important to their family.

Doctrinal issues seemed to have resulted from poor human relations and destroyed the fellowship of seemingly like minds. Poor human relation was in opposition to the biblical doctrine: love for God and for all humankind.

The fear of apostasy is also linked to fear of separation from God. This is a legitimate concern for many Christians. Fear will destroy all you have if you let it. Since apostasy is the rejection of Jesus Christ and His values, then all who are struggling to know God should be encouraged to keep that desire burning.

There may be times when the desire to know God may lead people down passionate paths of piety. Those paths may be different from those traditionally followed by members of your religious community. Will you abandon your faith because others expect you to provide sameness with their walks with God? The uniqueness of everyone's background and the motivation of the heart will determine the choice that leads toward or away from God. Separation from God is never accidental. It is always a choice. When the choice is not made to walk with God, permission is intentionally given for adversarial occupation.

> Who shall separate us from the love of Christ? shall tribulation, or distress, or persecution, or famine, or nakedness, or peril, or sword? As it is written, for thy sake we are killed all the day long; we are accounted as sheep for the slaughter. Nay, in all these things we are more than conquerors through him that loved us. For I am persuaded, that neither death, nor life, nor angels, nor principalities, nor powers, nor things present, nor things to come, nor height, nor depth, nor any other creature, shall be able to separate us from the love of God, which is in Christ Jesus our Lord. (Romans 8:35–39 AKJV)

The fear of abandonment by the Christian community may have led many to believe they have apostatized when they really haven't. A cautionary note is again sounded to the Christian world. Do not be quick to pass judgment on another when your experience with God is markedly different from theirs. It is better to provide reassurances for restoration than condemnations:

> Don't criticize, and then you won't be criticized. For others will treat you as you treat them. And why worry about a speck in the eye of a brother when you have a board in your own? Should you say, "Friend, let me help you get that speck out of your eye," when you can't even see because of the board in your own? Hypocrite! First get rid of the board. Then you can see to help your brother. (Matthew 7:1–5 TLB)

Every Christian should have a personal preference for the height at which they want to soar with God, the depth at which their root will be planted and the expanse of their faith. This should always remain a personal matter and a goal hungrily pursued for "Blessed are they which do hunger and thirst after righteousness: for they shall be filled" Matthew 5: 6 (AKJV). Even when another Christian is connected with you in prayer and in faith you petition the throne of God, the results of your intercession will be personal and should not be compared to the other.

God willingness to reveal himself to all humankind is always available. The Apostle John in relating messages for the revival and restoration for collective and individual walk with God declared:

> Behold, I stand at the door, and knock: if any man hears my voice, and open the door, I will come in to him, and will sup with him, and he with me. To him that overcometh will I grant to sit with me in my throne, even as I also overcame, and am set down with my Father in his throne. (Revelation 3:20–21 AKJV)

The fear of apostasy should be discredited in favor of God's promise to keep us from falling. Growing up in the Seventh-day Adventist Church, I was always fascinated at the instructional usage of scripture texts like Jude 24 (AKJV), especially at youth vesper's service. What intrigued me then was the reassurance that God can keep us from falling into sin. I have since realized that the application, though fitted for those times, always announced the sovereignty of God to maintain order in the life of every sinner who comes to Him in faith and believing.

I realized that the announcement of God's unlimited power was an intentional action of our leaders to plant in our hearts the omnipresence omniscience, and omnipotence of God. That God is still available today in the twenty-first century as he was in the twelfth century. So, the fear of apostasy will remain a real possibility throughout the sojourns of the Christian. The sojourner, however, has been assured of God's meaningful companionship along the way. The presence of God only intensifies adversarial attacks. Why fear when God is an ever-abiding presence?

> And now—all glory to him who alone is God, who saves us through Jesus Christ our Lord; yes, splendor and majesty, all power and authority are his from the beginning; his they are and his they evermore shall be. And he is able to keep you from slipping and falling away, and to bring you, sinless and perfect, into his glorious presence with mighty shouts of everlasting joy.
> Amen. (Jude 24–25 TLB)

The Christian should not fear apostasy because Jesus Christ saves to the uttermost those who accept the cost of discipleship (Hebrews 7:25 AKJV). The one who commits themselves to a spiritual journey with God will not be partially accepted, given second place, or abandoned along the way. Every disciple is fully accepted and given all the rights and privileges of salvation. The writer of the book of Hebrews penned it completely:

> Therefore, he is able to save completely those who come
> to God through him, because he always lives to intercede
> for them. (Hebrews 7:25 NET)

The testimonies of many who claim to be walking with God stand as impediments for those who desire to serve Him. Their report is one of impossibility, drudgery, doom, and gloom. Nothing about walking with God excites them. They reflect, in their words and deportment, a regretful walk with God and a low tolerance to a spiritual relationship that provides no advantage to their earthly lives. They don't associate with other professed disciples because their distance would reflect their disinterest, disbelief, and lack of conversion. As a matter of fact, they signal their relationship with God by saying, "Christianity is not easy. It's a sacrifice." Don't misunderstand me. Jesus addressed His journey to Jerusalem and, by extension, that of His disciples:

> If any man will come after me, let him deny himself, and
> take up his cross, and follow me. For whosoever will save
> his life shall lose it: and whosoever will lose his life for my
> sake shall find it. For what is a man profited, if he shall
> gain the whole world, and lose his own soul? or what shall
> a man give in exchange for his soul? (Matthew 16:24–26
> AKJV)

Jesus also emphasized the cost of discipleship, including family relations:

> If anyone comes to me and does not hate father and
> mother, wife and children, brothers and sisters—yes, even

their own life—such a person cannot be my disciple. And whoever does not carry their cross and follow me cannot be my disciple. (Luke 14:26–27 NIV)

There are costs that come with discipleship, but it is not the rejection of a better life for one that is dreary and suffocating. Discipleship demands total commitment and a prioritization of lifestyles. The Christian disciple is called to represent the values of Jesus Christ, but they do not become Jesus Christ. The Christian disciple does not become Christ in full or in part. Rather, the Christian disciple's life becomes an imitation of the values of Christ and a reflection of God's work on the heart. Therefore, everyone who accepts Jesus as Messiah and Savior of their lives will progressively but eventually reflect the manifestations of God's power in all their relationships.

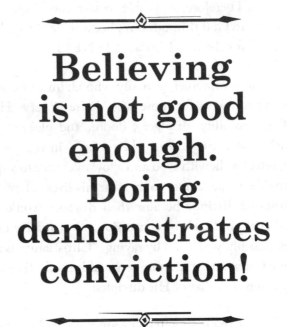

Believing is not good enough. Doing demonstrates conviction!

The Christian should not fear apostasy because there is security in God's hand. The Christian should not live in the fear that they are not safe in the arms of God and think they need to seek security elsewhere. That is anathema to the concept of trustworthiness in a relationship, particularly with God. There's a priceless comfort that comes with a trustworthy relationship. That comfort provides the level of security that ensures your vulnerability to the reference of your comfort and trust.

Nakedness is commonplace as the soul is exposed without reservation since trust envelops the relationship. The senses stay tuned to much-anticipated pleasantries. In that relationship, affirmation is standard, safety is immeasurable, integrity is wholesome, commitment is demonstrably confirmed, and acceptance is unconditional. Such an environment beckons much love—even unconditional love.

This is an imperfect description of the security that the Christian disciple has in Jesus Christ. It is unparalleled and unmatched by any type of relationship. We live each day to access that type of relationship with our family members, and we wonder if it is identifiable with friends. Maybe you have experienced it in your relationships. It is evident in God's love for humanity.

You see, humans are always seeking security. Humans need the capacity to breathe. Humans need to expand the capacity to breathe and live comfortably. All that desire is attached to a deeper desire to know that all will be well. Twentieth-century humanist and psychologist Abraham Maslow was convinced of that position. In 1943, he published a paper identifying a hierarchy of basic needs that human beings are instinctually motivated to satisfy before moving to more advanced needs in the quest for self-actualization. The most basic of all those needs are food, water, sleep, and warmth. Once those physiological needs have been met, people can move on to the next level of needs, which are for safety and security. According to that theory, behavior is significantly determined by the satisfaction of those needs.

Jesus emphasized that salvation is secured in Him. He emphasized the need to accept that security as an instrument of trust in His word. The guarantee of salvation is emphatically pronounced against existing doubts in the minds of desirable believers:

> Jesus answered, "I did tell you, but you do not believe. The works I do in my Father's name testify about me, but you do not believe because you are not my sheep. My sheep listen to my voice; I know them, and they follow me. I give them eternal life, and they shall never perish; no one will snatch them out of my hand. My Father, who has given them to me, is greater than all; no one can snatch them out of my Father's hand. I and the Father are one." (John 10:25–30 NIV)

Jesus said, "No one can snatch anyone given to me out of my hands or out of My Father's hand" (John 10:29 NIV). This should have you shouting! Fear—not apostasy. Ground yourself in the Word of God, and He will captain your salvation to safety.

Encouragement against Backsliding and Apostasy

A farmer went out to sow his seed. As he was scattering the seed, some fell along the path; it was trampled on, and the birds ate it up. Some fell on rocky ground, and when it came up, the plants withered because they had no moisture. Other seed fell among thorns, which grew up with it and choked the plants. Still other seed fell on good soil. It came up and yielded a crop, a hundred times more than was sown." When he said this, he called out, "Whoever has ears to hear, let them hear." His disciples asked him what this parable meant. He said, "The knowledge of the secrets of the kingdom of God has been given to you, but to others I speak in parables, so that 'though seeing, they may not see; though hearing, they may not understand.'" This is the meaning of the parable: The seed is the Word of God. Those along the path are the ones who hear, and then the devil comes and takes away the word from their hearts, so that they may not believe and be saved. Those on the rocky ground are the ones who receive the word with joy when they hear it, but they have no root. They believe for a while, but in the time of testing they fall away. The seed that fell among thorns stands for those who hear, but as they go on their way they are choked by life's worries, riches and pleasures, and they do not mature. But the seed on good soil stands for those with a noble and good heart, who hear the word, retain it, and by persevering produce a crop. (Luke 8:5–15 NIV)

When the Word of God is spoken to the heart of a sinner, referring to you and me, it is not guaranteed to transform our lives if we don't let it.

The deciding factor for making effective the work of heart obedience and character transformation is a commitment to be transformed. Just desiring transformation is incomplete in the work of salvation. The apostle James instructed us on the incompleteness of desirability against doing:

> Thou believest that there is one God; thou doest well: the devils also believe, and tremble. (James 2:19 AKJV)

There needs to be a commitment to the process of transformation and growth. This is how the seed takes root in the soil. Just the presence of the seed or the soil does not provide achievement. There's a need for a combination of efforts, such as a settling of the will, to produce from the potential within and to receive the much-needed resources from its environment.

One viable resource in the transformation process is the opportunity to grow. Opportunity for growth is always available. Life is always dynamic. Don't take your eyes off that reality. Failure to grow produces death. Other available resources include time, saturation, and resilience. The intention for sowing is always to reap and to reap bountifully. The expectation is that the seed will adequately produce according to its potential. Disappointment results when expectations are not met.

The failure of the seed to survive its environment can be compared to believers who don't survive the challenges of the journey with God. They gamble with their spiritual survival through their efforts to be in favor with worldly principles that weaken spirituality, and they are not true to their spiritual potential. They grow weak and become incapable of bearing after their spiritual kind. The efforts to identify with wrong principles, including non-biblical doctrines in an attempt to gain favor with the world, dwarfs the seed and leads to its death. Every effort must be made to be true to the intention of the sower and the potential of the seed, not forgetting the expectations of others to reap dividends from the production of the seed.

ASSESSMENT QUESTIONS

Have I taken time to understand that there is potential in me for transformative spiritual growth?

_____

_____

How committed am I to growing spiritually?

_____

_____

Am I backsliding from my spiritual values?

_____

_____

What do I think led to my spiritual backsliding?

_____

_____

Do I think others have a right to expect me to become a spiritually mature Christian?

_____

_____

If I haven't been backsliding, what keeps me from backsliding?

_____

_____

Take a moment and consider the distance you have walked without the company of Jesus.
What is an honest reason for welcoming Him back on the journey with you?

_____

_____

Do I believe in the saving grace of God though His Son, Jesus Christ, and by faith believe that the Son of God is all-sufficient to pardon my sins and restore me to a growing relationship with Him?

_____

_____

Apostasy is the total public rejection of Christianity as covenanted by baptism.

Heresy is the rejection of one or more Christian doctrines by one who professes an active adherence to Jesus Christ.

CHAPTER 13

The Appropriate Use of Fear

---◇---

My child, fear the Lord and the king. Don't associate with rebels, for disaster will hit them suddenly. Who knows what punishment will come from the Lord and the king?

—Proverbs 24:21–22 NLT

---◇---

Fear, the enemy, can and must be used to our advantage.
Knowing how to appropriately use fear has been a perennial challenge for many, including great achievers. The difference between a great achiever and a failure, both ferociously attacked by fear, is the courage to confront the emotion, the developing disposition, the false security, the tingling sensation of procrastination, the toleration of "having arrived, and the unusual abnormality to understand that fear is an adversarial element that needs no welcome. Remember, to live in fear is *not* of God.

Fear is the type of distractor that will not request an invitation to show up at your examination desk, swimming lesson, planning session, graduation ceremony, engagement proposal, promotion function, or wherever else you have the opportunity to shine. It is committed to intimidating you about your dreams, excitedly watching some slip through your fingers while jeering at you. Fear stalks the pursuer of great dreams. Fear unleashes tirades on the achiever and seeks to be compelling in its argument against ambitious desires. It is the epitome of the date that must not be flirted with or accepted because disappointment comes as an addition. Remember, God desires that we do *not* give in to the intimidation tactics of fear.

You may ask, "But what makes me so attractive to fear?"

Timidity attracts Fear. Don't cherish it. Banish it!

The answer? Timidity! Timidity is a magnetic attraction for fear. Without consent, fear shows up at all your life events because its presence has never been actively rejected. This indirect courtship that has not been canceled. A word in your lexicon, a chord in your character, or a movement in your behavior keeps signaling its presence. Hence, the lingering presence of distress in your life.

Silence is golden. This proverb can absolutely be applied as the solution to this dilemma. Silence is an implied invitation that can only be canceled with intentional actions. Not passivity. Consenting to live in fear can be as strongly implied as loudly as permission is spoken.

Fear will not vanish simply because you wish it will leave you alone. Action is the only proven magic wand that can vanish the adversarial element. Fear can be compared to an unhealthy relationship that is not going away—no matter how much you wish it would. You might pray to God, and it will begin to dissipate, but you're missing it so much that you grab at its heels and pull it right back to you. Everyone who wishes to be free from the vicious clutches of fear must motivate their soul to embrace the four pillars that will support their eternal escape: spirituality, intentionality, dedication, and commitment. These four pillars contain the antidote for the paralyzing drug that fear so willingly gives.

The Pillar of Spirituality

The foundation of every relationship is the value system upon which it is built. The foundation must be sufficiently strong to uphold the weighty challenges that will come to the relationship. In the spiritual dimension, the value system of the believer is anchored in the person of Jesus Christ. Spirituality, therefore, is companionship with God, the Creator and Ruler of all things.

In friendship with God, the only Spiritual Anchor for the believer, spiritual confidence fosters resilience in the life of the one who wishes to make God their companion. The connection—engendered through spiritual meditation, prayer, and favor of the relationship—will stimulate the much-needed passion for further spiritual growth. It is impossible to experience that spiritual connection if existing encumbrances are allowed to occupy the space that is needed for the indwelling presence of the friendship. Spiritual stagnation will result, and the relationship will lose favor and focus.

The intention of everyone who desires to be a disciple of Jesus Christ should be to use every opportunity to honor the consciousness of God in their lives and to be a channel through which His power can flow:

> The fear of the Lord tendeth to life: and he that hath
> it shall abide satisfied; he shall not be visited with evil.
> (Proverbs 19:23 KJV)

How this happens is contingent on your availability to be His instrument. To be God's instrument requires you to believe that He can bring out of you what He knows He planted in you to be a blessing to the world around you. To be God's instrument demands the abnegation of self from the thrones of complacency and conceitedness and a prostration at the feet of humility and service. Spirituality clarifies the purpose for the relationship and not the relationship seeking to define the composition of the foundation.

Spirituality speaks assertively to the tenets of trust, faith, hope in Jesus Christ. Trust is the relationship. Faith is the conductor of trust in the relationship. Hope is the platform for future benefits in the existing relationship. Spirituality cements the sojourner to the Foundation, Jesus Christ God's only divine Son, the anointed Messiah.

Solomon, the wisest man who ever lived, prescribes the manner to grow spiritually:

> Be not wise in thine own eyes: fear the Lord, and depart
> from evil. (Proverbs 3:7 KJV)

The heart that wishes to stand against fear must first be dedicated to its own spirituality.

The Pillar of Intentionality

This is the pillar that supports all who are experiencing doubtfulness in their walks with God. There is no substitute for it, and it cannot be eliminated from the mandatory needs of the spiritual sojourner. The pillar of intentionality stands boldly to inform all sojourners that there should be no wavering or doubt in the heart of the one who wishes to escape the destructive grip of fear. There must be purpose and deliberateness. There must be a purposeful movement toward the prized destination without succumbing to discomfort or pain. It is an absolute need.

There must be the desire to resist every opportunity to remain lifelessly chained to false promises or gazing at distant mirages of hope. The escape from those clutches demands that self-reliance be actively assessed and filtered for pseudo-agents with counterfeit hopes that are mimicking genuine productive agents.

The pillar of intentionality stands markedly different from all others and must not be mistaken for moodiness or mood swings. It stands to support the weakest soul seeking redemption from despair or false self-reliance. The soul must ask for both the desire to be intentional in self-assessment and to act intentionally.

Self-reliance must be consistently sourced outside of destructive agents, and it must guard against complacency and pride. Self-worship must be diminished, and focus must be placed on the spirituality, purpose, and destination of the relationship.

Being God's instrument requires that you believe He can bring out of you what he knows He planted in you for a blessing to the world around you.

The collaboration between self-assurance and competency must be intentionally pursued, for the sake of your relationship with God. Bear in mind that the motivation, willingness, or rejection of this pillar depends entirely on the level of trust you have in the relationship, your acceptance of its foundation, and your willingness to exercise faith in its Builder.

There can be no neutrality because neutrality stimulates fear, and fear ultimately motivates death. Fear's unassuming aim is to demotivate trust and interdependence in your relationship with God. By so doing, even God's best intention will be regarded as unfair, selfish, and impossible. Be intentional, therefore, and pursue the benefits of the

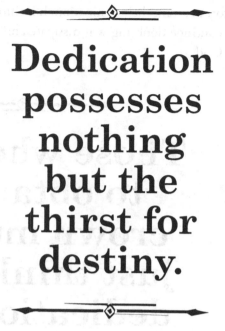

Dedication possesses nothing but the thirst for destiny.

relationship, focusing less on the challenges on the journey. Remember, you have God's promise that He will be with you until you have reached your destination.

The Pillar of Dedication

Every spiritual sojourner needs this pillar. Unfortunately, many fear its seemingly threatening demands. The Pillar of Dedication highlights to spiritual purpose, that leads to ultimate soul fulfillment. This is the attitude that exudes from the pillar of dedication. It calls loudly for the only decision that can make the spiritual journey enjoyable, which is the decision to unreservedly surrender the heart to God. You might not have the answers for future difficulties, but your dedication to purpose trumps all fears.

Dedication possesses nothing but the thirst for destiny. Therefore, the one who desires to obtain the crown must not just think about dedication; there must be a commitment to their effort to attain their destination. It is through self-discipline that the desire to continue doubting will dissipate and be replaced with hope and trust in God.

Those who desire to obtain the crown must not just think about dedication; they must display commitment to effort and attainment of that crown.

The pillar of dedication stands stately and tall against lingering doubt about the benefits of walking with God—even after experiencing abuse at the hands of fear. Many who claim to have a strong desire to endure their spiritual journeys lack much-needed dedication to the virtues that will carry them through unforeseen treacherous times. Every spiritual sojourner will discover that the dedication to endure until the end is not hitched to environmental seasons or physiological moods. It does not dance to the musical chants of personal preferences. Rather, it is entrenched in the blood of purpose, the sweat of dedication, and the tears of self-discipline.

The pillar of dedication stands as a perpetual rebuke to all accusations of inconsistencies that may be leveled at it. Every spiritual sojourner—even those who still battle with habits developed at the time of their relationship with fear—will discover that there is no better way to escape from the viciousness of fear than to intentionally dedicate the heart and all its potential to the successful completion of your walk with God.

The Pillar of Commitment

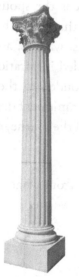

Fear of failing motivates those who are unwilling to commit. In the physical dimension, the staggering rate of divorce highlights a lack of commitment from one or both of the spouses. Likewise, in the spiritual dimension, failure to commit to walking with God because of fear will lead to colossal failure, the type of failure that is denominationally embarrassing, reputation defacing, and socially debilitating. Those types of failures include discontinuation of support for what was once accepted as biblical truth or acceptance of a more progressive lifestyle.

The pillar of commitment stimulates loyalty to God and a lifelong dedication to a spiritual lifestyle. It supersedes all other relationships, associations, fraternities, conventions, covenants, contracts, and related agreements. It is the pillar that emphasizes personal space more than any other virtue.

It emphasizes personal prayer life, personal Bible study, personal consciousness of life's purpose, personal goals and dreams, personal challenges, personal failures, and personal accomplishments. Spiritual consciousness is available to all who pursue it, but not every life will exude what is only received in personal time with God.

The pillar of commitment strengthens the sojourner who recognizes spiritual challenges, notes the treacherously intimidating meanderings of the journey, and does not surrender to its seemingly overwhelming demands. The spiritual sojourner does not fear the process. The spiritual sojourner walks determinedly to the end. That attitude epitomizes the biblical principle of spiritual resilience and enduring to the end:

> But he that shall endure unto the end, the same shall be saved. (Matthew 24:13 KJV)

The pillar of commitment exposes the weaknesses of many would-be greats, greats, failures, and aspiring achievers in every sector of life. The motivation for commitment is the same as all the other pillars. However, commitment is the specific motivation that establishes the promises made to those looking up to you.

The pillar of commitment is the motivation that keeps the spouse reaching out to the family despite existing challenges. It is that pillar that instills the discipline to reassess again and again what was, what is, and what needs to be. It is the pillar that provides much-needed inspiration to keep loving different personalities. It keeps parents bonded to their wayward children despite their embarrassing behaviors. Commitment does not deny its challenges; it prepares to accept them as part of the journey to that purposeful destination.

> Our happiness comes not from what is around us, but from what is within us; not from what we have, but from what we are.
> —*The Youth's Instructor*, January 23, 1902

ASSESSMENT QUESTIONS

How prepared am I to diminish fear's grip on my life?

_____

_____

Do I believe that I am less fearful about my walk with God today than I was yesterday?

_____

_____

How fulfilling is my faith in God?

_____

_____

What motivates my faith in God during difficult times?

_____

_____

Which pillar has been my weakest? My strongest?

_____

_____

What gives me the assurance that my walk with God is maturing?

_____

_____

In what ways have I demonstrated total reliance on God in difficult times?

_____

_____

CHAPTER 14

Conclusion

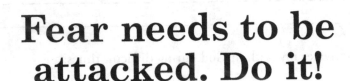

Fear needs to be attacked. Do it!

So, what is your plan of action?

What is your motivation to act against fear?

After what paradigm will you pattern your life?

To what degree will you make the necessary changes in your life?

We all must assertively respond to the above questions, because the outcome of our lives will be determined by the choices we keep making. Will we allow our future to be buffeted with trepidation and instability because we fear God has cursed us and/or our generation? Will it be a journey energized with the will, genius, and consciousness of the Divine?

We have assessed and experienced the traumatizing power of fear. We are now fully aware that fear is unfriendly to the ambitious, violent to the conscientious, demeaning to the respectful, dismissive of the focused, disruptive to the organized, flirtatious with the agreeable, and embracing of the laissez-faire. Anything you need for your success, in any dimension of your life, does not reside within the ambits of fear. Everything you need to fulfill God's will for your life resides on the other side of fear. Fear's threshold often occupies our lives, but we should not be afraid to go through fear because the promise that awaits us requires that we defeat its adversarial nature.

Men are disturbed not by things, but by the view which they take of them.

Epictetus

The Roman philosopher Epictetus said, "Men are disturbed not by things, but by the view which they take of them." Our view and acceptance of God will significantly impact our relationships with Him. Our views of God will define the appreciation of our spiritual experiences and our secular experiences. We would do well to develop a broader definition of trust and dependence upon God.

It would be to our benefit to adopt new meanings for fear and anxiety. We must strive to detoxify every dimension of our lives from fear. We must drain the debilitating effects of pessimism, fear, and anxiety from our souls.

We must accept that being stressed, worried, or anxious—and denying the impact of those emotions—have real health consequences that need to be understood, quantified, and incorporated into the management of fear on our spiritual journeys. As daunting as it may seem, the intentional application of faith will do much more to improve spiritual health than the existing paradigm of fearfulness.

Fear is intimidating. Acknowledge that. Understand that. Live with that awareness—but never live in fear of fear. Apply the awareness of God's presence to every area of your life. Fear nothing and no one. Live with that inner peace that comforts in times of distress. Disavow the control that fear is seeking on your life.

God is your Shepherd. He is with you on your spiritual journey. He will take you through whatever you need to go through to get you where He needs to get you. God will destroy the powers of your enemies through the means that He alone will receive honor. He is taking you through it so you will be able to say, "Though I walk through the valley of the shadow of death, I will fear no evil" (Psalm 23:4 AKJV).

Your Shepherd has the power to defend you, the wisdom to plan for you, the skills to equip you, the tools to provide successful passage through the valley of the shadow of all defeat, the ointment to disinfect your wounds, and the oil to anoint your body for your healing.

> Be strong and courageous. Do not be afraid or terrified
> because of them, for the Lord your God goes with you;
> he will never leave you nor forsake you. (Deuteronomy
> 31:6 NIV)

Everyone who desires to know God can do so. You sure can. Nothing has the capacity to change that. No one has control over that desire of yours. If you wish to experience the manifestation of God's power in your life, you can.

If you would like God to show up and show out in your business dealings, He can. He would love to be a lifetime supportive business partner. As a matter of spiritual promise, God desires you to dwell in His presence. He wants to be a permanent occupier of your territory. He desires to have a permanent seat at your table and to make the bounties of His grace elaborately available to you.

Apprehension often stands in the way of receiving the victories we need over fear. There is no reason for us to incapacitate our spiritual growth. Mistrust? Hesitation? Seasonal doubt? All of that can change when we wholeheartedly volunteer our fear to God. Fear has reigned in your life and mine for much too long. It has occupied territory that could have produced the best of fruit for the advancement and nourishment of all our lives. It occupied that space and imprinted its name on the foundation that you built. It was saying, "I have a right to occupy that building. My name is in the foundation." Please don't let this happen to you.

Everything you need to fulfill God's will for your life, resides on the other side of fear.

Fear is waiting to ambush you. Its objective is to immobilize you. Fear will obliterate that dream of yours if you let it. Fear is seeking to stop you from becoming more than just a human who occupied time and experienced anxieties from birth to death. Will you let fear attack and phase you out—or will you attack it and terminate its agenda? Attack it now! Attack it today! Attack fear like your life depends on it. Attack fear as if it is your last chance to do it because now is all you have. Unimproved opportunities can result in despair. Attack fear with everything you have within you. Do so while noting the inspiration of the scriptures: "God has *not* given to us a spirit of fear" (2 Timothy 1:7 AKJV).

If He didn't give it, where did it come from? Who gave it to you? Where did you pick it up? Who dropped it in your bag as you went shopping for spiritual virtues? Now is the ideal time to do something about the destructive trend that fear is creating in you. In the strength of God, get up and attack that fortress called fear. Attack it head-on! Attack it with a plan! You don't have the option of waiting because the adversary will fortify its walls against your attacks. That fort will only become more difficult to conquer.

Love God. Don't live in fear of Him. Trust God. Don't ostracize Him. Get up close and personal with God. Share with Him—as you have not done with any other—the secrets of your enlightened or darkened heart. He is able to deal with the contents. No revelation will disturb His equilibrium, erase His memory, destabilize His authority, or change the trajectory of His rulership. Trust Him! Get God out of that box you have built and recognize His omnipotence in the minutest existence of your world.

Fear must be dethroned. Your purpose should not be stifled by the presence of fear in your life or its adamance to stay on the throne of your heart. Many would beat themselves up and let fear stop them from achieving their dreams. Shamefully, they do not realize that if they attack and eliminate fear from their lives, they would be happy and progressive. Are you willing to make it happen?

Fear's occupation, through ill-advised, has outlived its time. It's your time now. It's urgent.

It's time to fear not and worship more.

It's time that others are told about the veracity and character of fear. Expose fear for what it is.

It's time to apply the words of Jesus in their entirety and not in partiality.

It's time that potential speaks louder than comfort and tolerance.

It's time to take some action to cancel fear and not promote it.

It's time that spiritual virtues are seen as benefits and not hindrances to greatness.

It's time to understand that the seed of greatness in you is not the same as the fruit you can bear.

It's time to realize that desire bears no fruit and that the seed must be in the soil.

It's time to live life fully.

It's time for bearing fruit.

It's time that the ground on which fear stands be shaken by the movement of greatness coming to its rightful position.

It's time that your soul experiences the strong wind of success blowing across the dwarfed trees of the valley.

It's time to recognize that *later* can become *never*. Never plan on later. Now is what you have! Fear not!

It's time to understand that God is asking for your time to mesh with His plan for your life. Develop that consciousness of God and live the revelations rewarded you.

It's time that your spiritual journey is refreshed with the manifestations of God in the past and the expectation for greater manifestations in the future.

Never surrender your waiting victory for a pot of refreshing fear. If comfort is all you want, you can easily attain that without doing anything meaningful. If you will not oppose the seduction of retreat because the journey is too costly, then you can, without persuasion, surrender your potential to the oppositional voices. If you desire to serve a legacy of tenacious courage to the pantheons of faithful Christians cheering you on to victory, you must fight fear boldly with the knowledge that there will be gruesome moments in the hope of victory. If that fear emboldens its tenacity to increase the odds of your defeat, fight on! It's better to nurse a wound because of courage than to perish because of fear.

As you shape your future walk with God, I urge you to become more conscious of yourself and the hindrance that self-reliance can pose in your journey with Him. The shapeless structure of time will carve out an experience that you can only appreciate if you trust in God. The opinions of others will be matter less when you are convicted of the virtuous goal of becoming all that God wants you to be. Don't worry. You will know what He wants you to be because He's willing to reveal the information to you along the way.

Frown on every attempt to dissuade you from walking with God. Critique every recommendation that does not promote His consciousness in your life. Dismiss the ideological presupposition that God has no interest in your future and has left you with the careless choice of inconsequence for whatever you wish to do.

Every sojourner will have to answer this question: "Am I able to spiritually benefit from a relationship with God if I am afraid of Him?" If the answer is contrary, then the principles of this book will become crucially important in your triumphant journey; otherwise, dismiss the content of this text as ideologically irrelevant to the spiritual sojourner. I am convinced, however, that the imperative to call upon God and the privilege to walk with Him will continue to be spiritually fulfilling and a timeless heritage as we cast fear out of that sacred space called life. What will it be for you?

In the strength of God Almighty, I encourage you to not fail or falter. Do not grow weary or tired. Unflinchingly move forward amid the sound of invading distractions. Let not the relentless attacks of discouragement or the loudness of dissenting voices wear you down. God has given you the tools! Now accept the calling and fearlessly get the job done.

> Fear ye not me? saith the Lord: will ye not tremble at my presence, which have placed the sand for the bound of the sea by a perpetual decree, that it cannot pass it: and though the waves thereof toss themselves, yet can they not prevail; though they roar, yet can they not pass over it? (Jeremiah 5:22 AKJV)

> When you go out to war against your enemies and see horses, chariots, and an army larger than yours, do not be afraid of them; for the Lord your God, who brought you out of the land of Egypt, is with you. (Deuteronomy 20:1 NIV)

ASSESSMENT QUESTIONS

Do I have the courage to attack my fears?

_____

_____

What are my greatest fears?

_____

_____

What are my smallest fears?

_____

_____

Which of my fears are motivated by my religious beliefs?

_____

_____

What am I prepared to do in order to get rid of my fears?

_____

_____

On a scale of one to ten, rate your motivation to obliterate your fears. (The closer you get to ten, the more motivated you are).

_____

_____

Do I have faith that I can expunge my fears? If yes, what is my history of exercising faith in God?

_____

_____

Reflections

Happiness is not pursued; it is discovered. It is not without us; but within us. When we reach to the core of our souls, and make use of the potential that lies within us—despite what is around us or seeking to distract us— nothing but creative excitement will spring from within us. From our bosoms rises the reassurance that our Creator is actively seeking to reach us, to bless us with all that will sustain us, and position us where only God's grace can enrich us. Happiness is being safely anchored, positioned, unafraid, secured, and satisfied that we live to honor God who lives to have us honored.

As you plan for tomorrow, hoping for the best to come, remember to celebrate the small victories, because they account for your resolve. Note your progress and give yourself an advantage, by delighting in what you've done. Add to today's achievements the motivation to remain resilient and in dogged pursuit of what has already been promised to you.

The predictable truth is that the waves will hit against the sailing ship. You can choose to go back to the harbor and stay securely anchored,—or you can sail out and do what ships are made to do.

*Fear not, for I
am with you.
Do not be dismayed.
I am your God. I will
strengthen you; I
will help you; I will
uphold you with my
victorious right hand.
(Isaiah 41:10 TLB)*

Enthusiasm
is the consistent
injection of courage,
resilience, and hope
in the face of adversity.

Resilience is moving from potential failure to intentional success without acceding to seeming hopelessness.

*W*hen you feel afraid, resolve
in your will to trust in God.
Asking for comfort is asking for
ease—thoughtful and predictable—
as all would think they need.
Remember, sojourner, that every traveler
is set on a journey and charting a
path—often with no footprints of others
to follow. It is exactly what others shun
since there seems to be no tomorrow.
What needs to be known is that others
will follow, when there is commitment
and a chance for tomorrow.
Sojourner, the path is formed with
every step you take, and direction
is given though silently spoken.
The more you walk in that direction,
the more distinct the path you create,
for those behind you to see and follow.
Choose therefore, to create a path, where
other travelers will look and observe
a committed leader with nothing but
courage and no fear of tomorrow.

REFERENCES

Authorized King James Version (AKJV). KJV reproduced by permission of Cambridge University Press, the Crown's patentee in the UK.

Berean Study Bible (BSB). Reproduced by Bible Hub and Berean Bible 2016, 2018. Used by permission. All rights reserved.

Britannica, T. Editors of Encyclopaedia (February 10, 2021). Salt. Encyclopedia Britannica. https://www.britannica.com/science/salt-acid-base-reactions.

Brown-Driver-Briggs Hebrew and English Lexicon, Unabridged, Electronic Database.

Copyright 2002, 2003, 2006 by Biblesoft, Inc. All rights reserved. Used by permission. BibleSoft.com.

Chisholm, Thomas O. Music by William M. Runyan (c) 1923, Ran. 1951 Hope Publishing Co., Carol Stream, IL 60188. www.hopepublishing.com. All rights reserved. Used by permission.

Danieli, Y., Norris, F., and Engdahl, B. (2017). "A Question of Who, Not If: Psychological Disorders in Holocaust Survivors' Children." *Psychological Trauma: Theory, Research, Practice, and Policy*, 98–106. doi: 10.1037/tra00s0192.

https://www.brainyquote.com/quotes/aristotle_118588.

https://www.cerealsgrains.org/publications/plexus/cfw/pastissues/2008/Documents/.

CFW-53-1-0004.pdf, Role of Salt in Baking.

https://en.wikipedia.org/wiki/Great_Is_Thy_Faithfulness.

https://files.eric.ed.gov/fulltext/ED501708.pdf.

https://www.goodreads.com/quotes/321104-inch-by-inch-life-s-a-cinch-yard-by-yard-life-s.

https://hymnary.org/text/god_of_mercy_and_compassion_look_with_pi

https://iep.utm.edu/nietzsch/

http://www.mesacc.edu/~barsp59601/text/philtext/plato/laches.html.

https://newspaperarchive.com/bar-harbor-times-jul-11-1940-p-3/.

https://positivepsychology.com/abraham-maslow/.

https://quotestemple.com/quote-id/2514/.

Longfellow, Henry, Wadsworth. https://www.poetryfoundation.org/poets/ henry-wadsworth-longfellow.

Living Bible (TLB). The Living Bible copyright 1971 by Tyndale House Foundation. Used by permission of Tyndale House Publishers Inc., Carol Stream, Illinois 60188. All rights reserved.

Miller, R. A., Hoseney, R.C. Kansas State University, Manhattan, KS. R & R Research Services, Inc., Manhattan, KS. *Cereal Foods World* 53:4–6.

Moccia L, Mazza M, Di Nicola M, Janiri L. "The Experience of Pleasure: A Perspective between Neuroscience and Psychoanalysis." *Front Hum Neurosci*. 2018; 12:359. doi:10.3389/fnhum.2018.00359.

Naeem, F., Swelam, M., and Kingdon, D. (2012). "Introduction: CBT and the Culture." In F. Naeem and D. Kingdon (Eds.), *Psychology Research Progress*. "Cognitive Behaviour Therapy in Non-Western Cultures" (1–14). Nova Science Publishers.

New Century Bible (NCV). The Holy Bible, New Century Version. Copyright 2005 by Thomas Nelson, Inc.

New English Translation (NET). The Holy Bible, NET Bible copyright 1996–2017 by biblical Studies Press, L.L.C. http://netbible.com All rights reserved.

New International Version (NIV). The Holy Bible, New International Version, NIV Copyright 1973, 1978, 1984, 2011 by Biblica, Inc. Used by permission. All rights reserved worldwide.

New King James Version (NKJV). Scripture taken from the New King James Version. Copyright 1982 by Thomas Nelson. Used by permission. All rights reserved.

New Living Translation (NLT) Holy Bible. New Living Translation, copyright 1996, 2004, 2015 by Tyndale House Foundation. Used by permission of Tyndale House Publishers, Inc., Carol Stream, IL 60188. All rights reserved.

New Revised Standard Version (NRSV) New Revised Standard Version Bible, copyright 1989 the Division of Christian Education of the National Council of the Churches of Christ in the United States of America. Used by permission. All rights reserved.

William, Clark (2000) *Scientific American*, https://www.scientificamerican.com/article/Is our tendency to experience fear and anxiety genetic?.

"The Legacy of Trauma." (2020). Retrieved from https://www.apa.org/monitor/2019/02/legacy-trauma.

White, Ellen G. 6LtMs, Ms 42, 1890, South Lancaster, MA.

White, Ellen G. (1908). *The Desire of Ages*. Signs of the Times Publishing Association, Warburton, Victoria.

White, Ellen G. (1933). *Education*. Signs Publishing Co.: Warburton, Victoria.

White, Ellen G. (1979). *Faith and Works*. Southern Publishing Association, Nashville, TN.

White. Ellen G. (1885). *Review and Herald*. Review and Herald Publishing Association, Battle Creek, MI.

White, Ellen. G. *The Youth's Instructor*, January 23, 1902. Review and Herald Publishing Association, Battle Creek, MI.

Courage is the unrelenting application of hope in the face of daunting adversity.